Costume Design

FilmCraft

Costume Design

Deborah Nadoolman Landis

ELSEVIER

AMSTERDAM • BOSTON • HEIDELBERG • LONDON
NEW YORK • OXFORD • PARIS • SAN DIEGO
SAN FRANCISCO • SINGAPORE • SYDNEY • TOKYO

Focal Press is an imprint of Elsevier

**Focal
Press**

Focal Press is an imprint of Elsevier Inc.
225 Wyman Street, Waltham
MA 02451, USA
Copyright © 2012 The Ilex Press Ltd.
All rights reserved

This book was conceived, designed, and produced by
Ilex Press Limited, 210 High Street, Lewes, BN7 2NS, UK

Publisher: Alastair Campbell
Associate Publisher: Adam Juniper
Managing Editors: Natalia Price-Cabrera and Zara Larcombe
Editor: Tara Gallagher
Specialist Editor: Frank Gallaugher
Creative Director: James Hollywell
Senior Designer: Kate Haynes
Design: Grade Design
Picture Manager: Katie Greenwood
Color Origination: Ivy Press Reprographics

ISBN: 978-0-240-81866-5
For information on all Focal Press publications visit our website at:
www.focalpress.com
Printed and bound in China
10 9 8 7 6 5 4 3 2 1

Table of Contents

Introduction

I am delighted to be the editor of *FilmCraft: Costume Design* and to have the opportunity to introduce some of today's most gifted designers to you. With the exception of the "Legacy" chapters, the costume designers profiled here are all working professionals. Most were actively involved in a current production when I contacted them to be interviewed. Although they struggled to schedule a time to talk, each generously shared their personal history, their war stories and their design philosophy. The artwork in *FilmCraft: Costume Design* was loaned from the designers' personal portfolios, most drawings are published here for the very first time.

The role of the costume designer is really quite simple: costume designers design the people in the movie. Our contribution to the story is more profound than providing the clothes for a production. The word "costume" works against us. The word is vulgar when what we do is incredibly refined. "Costume" is invariably associated with Halloween, fancy dress, parade, theme park, Mardi Gras, carnival, and the clothes in fantasy and period films. To costume designers, "a costume picture" means nothing more than our next project. Adding to the confusion by the industry and the public about our role is an uncertainty about the fundamental purpose of costume design. Film costuming serves two equal purposes: the first is to support the narrative by creating authentic characters (people); and the second is composition, to provide balance within the frame by using color, texture, and silhouette.

In addition to the creation of the authentic people in the movie, costume designers also help paint each "frame" of film. If the dialogue is the melody of a movie, the color provides the harmony, a satisfying visual cohesiveness or "style." It's imperative for the designers on a film to have a strong reference point from which to create a style. Beyond the panniers of Marie Antoinette and the exaggerations of any period silhouette, every costume adds texture and color to a scene. The choices for a designer abound. In fact, designers complain that contemporary costuming presents "too many" choices. Some designers prefer the stark simplicity of the flat planes of solid color fabric, while others prefer using multiple patterns and find it the key to layering character. Designers may alter their approach with the feel of the project and make adjustments to accommodate the style of the director. The modern hoodie sweatshirt, like Eddie Murphy's red hoodie in my design for **Trading Places** (1983), Mark Bridges' gray hoodie for Eminem in **8 Mile** (2002), and Michael Kaplan's black hoodie for Tom Cruise in **Mission: Impossible—Ghost Protocol** (2011) is the contemporary answer to the hip man's hat and jacket. Framing the face and focusing our attention to an actor's most important feature— his eyes—hoodies underscore their dialogue. Color is a powerful tool that directors and costume designers leverage to support the narrative and create a unified fictional space. Color telegraphs emotion in a scene to the audience as quickly as the musical score. And a costume has to move—designers work in a kinetic art.

A successful costume must be subsumed by the story and be woven seamlessly into the narrative and visual tapestry of the movie. Aggie Guerard Rodgers put it this way: "I want the clothes to not get in the way of the writer's words." Even in the Hollywood style of the 1930s, which was considered realistic by the 1920s standards, motion pictures could not survive one glamorous entrance after another. Movies are not fashion shows that runway models perform with a blank stare; there is a reason that they are called "mannequins." They are the human hangers for a fashion designer's imagination. Costumes, like the characters they embody, must evolve within the context of the story and the arc of the character within it. Hollywood has suffered through the poor choice of spectacle over story again and again. From the early epics, which were top-heavy with gaudy sets and bejeweled extras, to today's super-hero special effects extravaganzas, Hollywood has always been tempted to show too much. Certainly, costume design has a place in cinema spectacle, but what the audience remembers and what stays forever, is a great movie regardless of the number of people (or what they are wearing) on screen. Whatever the budget, the best movies transport the audience. Suspension of disbelief is complete when the audience "notices" nothing and is entirely immersed in the story.

Every costume in a motion picture, whether it's David Fincher's **Fight Club** (1999, designer Michael Kaplan) or John Sayles' **Lone Star** (1996, designer Shay Cunliffe), was created for a certain moment in the arc of a film, to be lit in a certain way, to be seen on one set, on one actor. Costumes in the movies are made for that moment by the designer to fulfill the needs of the director and the screenplay. In modern comedy and drama the clothes will not be noticed but they will affect the audience. **Lone Star** is an ensemble piece with multiple concurrent stories. Sayles wove that complex narrative into a brilliant tale and depended on Cunliffe to create characters that we can instantaneously recognize without confusion. Fincher's **Fight Club** is the story of a personality split in two, embodying the sexy Tyler Durden and the uptight Narrator. Kaplan has said that their contrasting clothes looked like they were created for two different films. These exquisite examples of the art of costume design can only exist in the universe of modern costuming. It is the place where the audience can recognize the character as a person they may know or may be. The subtleties of the costume design are well beyond the cut of a period sleeve; they reach into the very soul of the character.

Many of the designers in this volume have enduring partnerships with their directors. Mark Bridges is currently designing his sixth movie with Paul Thomas Anderson. They have been working together for 16. Bridges says, "That doesn't mean it's without occasional tensions." Joanna Johnston, a long-time Spielberg stalwart, agrees, "I love working for new directors, too, but I love the trust you get from the director that you've worked with before." Janty Yates is currently at work on her seventh movie for Ridley Scott. Working with the same director creates a shorthand and saves precious time. In the pressure cooker that is modern film pre-production, the value of having a pre-existing relationship with a director makes an exponential difference in what a costume designer can produce in a very short time. Confidence in their ability to second-guess a director may allow a designer to take a risk with a character or a costume that they would otherwise play safe in a new professional relationship.

Costumes are one of the tools a filmmaker has to tell a story. A designer's challenge is to realize the director's vision and to bring that script (and that moment) to the screen. No script, no set, no costumes. A designer's work is inextricable from the theatrical context and collaborative interrelationships in which they work—the dialogue, the actor, the cinematography, the weather, the season, the time of day, the choreography of movement and a dozen other dilemmas all present challenges. Judianna Makovsky said, "It's funny. A lot of directors aren't necessarily interested in the clothes…they're more interested in the character and the visuals of the whole world." Wise directors use film designers to articulate the visual world of the screenplay. Communication is the key—directors must tell us what they want. Costume designers and production designers don't work in a vacuum. A designer's work exists to actualize the screenplay—defining the people and the places, a marriage of concept and imagery. That's why it's called the language of film design. Designers love a director who's a collaborator, somebody who inspires us to do our best work. Sometimes, directors and designers get pegged in a genre when a conventional wisdom dictates that period and fantasy films require a specialist. Mary Zophres remembers when, "…after **The Big Lebowski** (1998) the Coens called: 'We're going to do this movie called, **Oh, Brother Where Art Thou**.' A lot of directors in Hollywood would have gone to a designer who had designed a 1930s' movie. It didn't even occur to them. They feel that I'm capable of designing anything that they write."

The career of the motion-picture costume designer, with few exceptions, is dominated by the design of modern films. All designers bounce back and forth between genre and budget, every project presents a different challenge. There is an industry-wide confusion regarding the use of stylists and the product placement of fashion and accessories, promoted heavily in fashion magazines to please their advertisers. A designer's choice for a garment or accessory on any modern project is based upon what the character's choices would be in their own life. Our "art imitates life." No one buys all their clothes at the same shop on the high street or in the mall in one day and neither do the characters in the movies. Real people don't use stylists, →

celebrities do. People do not wear Tom Ford and Marc Jacobs from head to toe every day, and neither do the people in the movies. We all wear a mix and match of clothes that are old favorites and new purchases, clothes that are bought and borrowed, and accessories that are inheritances and gifts. Every single thing that we wear has its own story. We expect our on-screen characters to be the same. Most urgently, the actor must adopt them for her or his own. The clothes and the people must ring true.

Fashion design sometimes is a plot point like in **Sabrina** (1954). Sabrina (Audrey Hepburn) disappears to Paris to go to cooking school and arrives home after an extreme makeover with a trunk full of Hubert de Givenchy's best gowns. In this case, with the permission of the brilliant director, Billy Wilder, the "look" takes center stage and the clothes do the acting for Miss Hepburn. Her new wardrobe reflects her transformation; she has "grown up" in Paris. The dramatic result is unforgettable. **The Devil Wears Prada** (2006, designer Patricia Field) is another Cinderella story that uses clothes (and the ludicrousness of fashion) as the engine for the narrative. Patricia Field's costumes work hard for the comedy and the plot. Yvonne Blake explains the role of the designer on a modern film this way: "For me costume design and fashion are two very, very different elements. I'm trying to create a person. I study the psychology of this person and why they should be dressed in this way. There's just so much that a designer needs to 'get right.' Costumes embody the psychological, social, and emotional condition of the character at a particular moment in the script. It is impossible to design for the actor unless the designer knows who the character is."

Costume designers consider modern films to be more complicated than lavish period projects. However, like the popular myth of actors improvising their dialogue, modern costumes— everyday clothes—are taken for granted by the public and the film industry. Since everyone gets dressed in the morning, everyone considers themselves an expert on contemporary clothes. For the film to work the audience must be able to say, absolutely, "I recognize that person." Julie Weiss agrees: "I learned that my job is to show the audience people who look like somebody

they know. In this business there are designers that I admire who know how to do the glamour. I've been trained to do that too. But something happens to me when an actor merges with who their character is and then everything gets rained on. That's when I know I can help, no matter what the year or the period." Film design today is approached with a greater emphasis on accuracy and faithfulness to the script and to research than ever before.

High or low budget, all motion pictures utilize a combination of bought, rented and manufactured costumes. The idea that modern costumes are "shopped" for by designers on Madison Avenue or Bond Street boutiques, reaching the screen unaltered with fashion designers' labels intact, is a popular myth promoted by the fashion industry. When a fashion designer's garment does appear on screen it is billboarded and heavily publicized. Often a separate "product placement" contract has been signed between the studio and the label with cash from the label to offset production costs. This is not the optimal way to design a movie. Time is the designer's enemy and running to a late-night mall when casting is late and a shooting deadline looms is sometimes a designer's only option. Optimally, a costume designer will alter, refit, dye and age all modern clothes. A designer's greatest test is to mix them up and make the labels disappear. Sharen Davis adds, "It's very hard to talk down some actresses about high-fashion design. It is the lure of the label. For me, contemporary costume is a challenge—it is the highest level of creativity because I have to come up with the character's own original look." A designer's work is about getting toward the center (the spirit) of the character and finding out who that person is— whether the clothes are made, shopped or picked off the floor of the actor's closet. Fashion designers often credit classic and current movies as influencing their style, although they rarely credit the costume designer. But it's not the clothes they are inspired by. Like the audience, they are seduced by the story, by the movie, and the glamour ignited by the elixir of fascinating characters, imbued with the charismatic personalities of the actors. It is captivating people in sexy stories that set the style, in the scripts written by invisible screenwriters, played by shape-shifting actors, designed by costume designers serving directors who are relentlessly seeking the truth. Setting fashion trends is the last thing designers have on their minds when making movies. The fact that films are released about one year after they have finished shooting makes it nearly impossible for costume designers to be deliberate about influencing fashion. First, the audience must fall in love with the story. Michael Kaplan remembers, "When **Flashdance** (1983, Michael Kaplan) came out the trend was on the cover of *Time* magazine, but they never once mentioned the costume designer of the movie. It's never my intention to start any kind of a trend. A director once said to me, 'We want you to set a trend the same way you did for **Flashdance**.' I said, 'Well, you know you have responsibility in this too.' He said, 'Really?' I said, 'Yes, the movie has to be a huge hit.'" Fashion trends are created by movies and characters that connect with the audience, whether the movie is **Flashdance**, **Annie Hall** (1977, designer Ruth Morley) or **Wall Street** (1987, designer Ellen Mirojnick). Only the public determines if a movie will be a hit or a flop. Designers work with the same enthusiasm and commitment on every project.

Over the last decade there has been compression in the pre-production of motion pictures. It is true that there have also been tremendous changes in technology. Costume designers are major users of smartphones and tablet computers as time savers. These hand-held devices shorten the time between the question and the answer at the office, on the set, in the fitting room or at the fabric shop; red or yellow, patterned or plain, short or long, cotton or wool? Costume designers scan fabrics and send PDFs and Photoshopped fitting photos to directors, producers and executives at a studio half a world away. Physical research bibles have been eclipsed by websites created by designers to make research available at any time to the creative team or their cast to browse. It's very rare that a designer has the time now to sit at a drafting table to draw, and costume illustrators have become their public letter-writers—if there is even time in pre-production to supervise costume sketches, and often there isn't time.

Our role on a film has not changed significantly since the time that our "Legacy" designers were working in our field. But the film industry has changed.

Costume design has always been stressful. Even during the heyday of MGM in the Golden Age of Hollywood there has never been "enough" money or "enough" time to do the job correctly. Every designer included in *FilmCraft: Costume Design* mentioned the significant change in the industry over the past ten years. Shay Cunliffe explains the increasing strain on the job: "There is stress on big-budget films and there is a multiplying number of opinions that we deal with that are highly stressed about the amount of money that they're investing in a project." Many designers have emailed fitting photos to executives and producers who they have never met and whose role on the film is unclear. Late casting on films is an industry hazard and designers often have to cope with an actor cast on Sunday who needs to be dressed and ready on the set early Monday morning. This regrettable practice has become commonplace. Shay continues: "It takes no less time to create that costume. Not one minute less time to figure out in a fitting, to source the fabric and to have it made." When we arrive at work at 5 a.m., designers are prepared for long days and to engage in trench warfare. It is intense. Joanna Johnston reflects that, "Costume design in films is somewhere between the circus and a war—and can flip flop between that sometimes on an hourly or a daily basis."

Designing people is the role of a "key" collaborator, but to this day the Directors Guild of America does not list the costume designer in the *DGA* magazine with the listed cinematographer, production designer and editor, all of whom are credited on a production. This longtime omission at the DGA perpetuates the nefarious gender bias in the industry. In addition, the salary of costume designers is not comparable with the other key collaborators. Our minimum is tied to a union contract hidebound by long-standing precedent with the studios. In fact, in the current agreement the base salary for the costume designer is nearly one third less than an entering production designer. Benchmarking salaries does not exist. →

Internationally, the weekly wage of the costume designer does not approach the minimums of the cinematographer, production designer and editor. Whether practiced by women or by men, costume design has always been considered "women's work" and is paid (and valued) commensurately less. It may also be a surprise that cinema costume designers are "work for hire." Cinema costume designers do not own their sketches, or the costumes, and jewelry they design. They receive no credit or compensation for copies made from their designs for action figures and dolls, Halloween costumes, or fashion lines.

Professional costume designers want the world to understand what we do. I believe that much of the confusion surrounding our role as key collaborators can be addressed by educating filmmakers. Undergraduate and graduate theater programs offer costume design as part of the conservatory-style rotation and where theater directors (like the young Francis Ford Coppola at UCLA) may intern in the costume shop. With the exception of the emerging unified program at the UCLA School of Theater, Film and Television, costume design is absent in film producing and directing programs. Costuming for student films is universally trivialized and an afterthought. University film programs must include a fully integrated film design curriculum as part of their core curriculum. A conservatory approach mirrors professional film production where a dozen crafts work in unison. The benefits are exponential; when talented filmmakers enter the industry they will produce more complex and more beautiful movies. Filmmakers will understand that characters don't just walk onto the stage fully formed; they look that way by design. My filmmaking students are often surprised by the powerful contribution of the costume designer to cinematic iconography. I point out my design for Indiana Jones, Judianna Makovsky's design for Harry Potter, and Penny Rose's design for Captain Jack Sparrow. Many student directors simply have no idea what goes into the creation of memorable character but are excited by how intelligent costuming can add depth to their films. Movies are about people and that's what costume designers do.

There are treasures in this book. The number of interwoven lives, careers, and stories was a completely unexpected bonus. Many designers started their career at Barbara Matera Costumes in New York and at Bermans and Nathans Costumiers in London. Although these chapters span two generations and a wide geographic and economic sphere, the journey to the profession of costuming is not dissimilar. All of these designers were singled out as talents at an early age. Every designer knew at once that they were different and each understood that they possessed a special gift. Most were recognized by their parents as unique and supported in their schooling and artistic careers. Some started by assisting legendary designers like Milena Canonero and Anthony Powell and many assisted established designers like Richard Hornung and Judy Ruskin. Others began as theater designers and cinema costume supervisors, and a few arrived from the fashion world after an epiphany that led them to costume design.

Splendidly, most of the costume designers here were helped by a generous referral from their mentors. There was an instant in each of their lives when their mentor chose not to take a design assignment and a new career was ignited by that opportunity. The designers' generosity to each other is overwhelming. Barbara Matera and Max and Monty Berman often referred their favorite house assistants and costumers for design work. It must be said that this kindness was also practiced at Western Costume Company and the costume houses in California. Ange Jones, the chief of the NBC Costume Department, was my own guardian angel. The costume designer Julie Weiss was mentioned in three chapters by Shay Cunliffe, Michael Kaplan and Aggie Guerard Rodgers, and her influence is widely felt among a generation of designers. The designers in this volume are united by a multiplicity of passions: history, literature, theater, gardening, fashion, and the movies. Maurizio Millenotti speaks for the group when he remembers that as a child, "Movies were an utter marvel. I was enchanted by that world of adventure and lavishness."

The pool of incredible talent in the field of costume design is expanding exponentially. We represent a legion of inspired international film artists. Colleen Atwood (in 2011, designing two films simultaneously) could easily publish her own monograph. Joe Aulisi, Kym Barrett, John Bloomfield, Consolata Boyle, Alexandra Byrne, Eduardo Castro, William Chang, Chen Changmin, Phyllis Dalton, Ngila Dickson, John Dunn, Jacqueline Durran, Marie France, Louise Frogley, Danny Glicker, Julie Harris, Betsy Heimann, Deborah Hopper, Gary Jones, Renee Ehrlich Kalfus, Charles Knode, Ruth Myers, Michael O'Connor, Daniel Orlandi, Beatrix Aruna Pasztor, Karen Patch, Janet Patterson, Arianne Phillips, Sophie de Rakoff, Tom Rand, May Routh, Mayes Rubeo, Rita Ryack, Deborah Scott, Anna B. Shepard, Marlene Stewart, Huamiao Tong, Tracy Tynan, Emi Wada, Jacqueline West, and Michael Wilkinson among many others could easily fill the next ten *FilmCraft* companion volumes. If it was very difficult to decide who to include in this book, imagine my dilemma regarding the choices for the five "Legacy" chapters. I need more room! Theoni V. Aldredge, Marit Allen, Milo Anderson, Andre-Ani, Donfeld, Piero Gherardi, Julie Harris, Richard Hornung, Orry-Kelly, Anna Hill Johnstone, Bernard Newman, Dolly Tree, Natalie Visart, and Vera West represent just a tiny fraction of the incredible cinema designers whose careers merit books in themselves, but who remain largely anonymous to even the most devoted film fans. Today, our colleagues all over the world are creating characters, igniting fashion trends, expanding popular culture and making cinematic history.

Some of the costume designers included in this volume are close friends; and there are others who I look forward to meeting in person. I remain a fan simply in awe of the beauty of their work and of their dedication and commitment. Most of the designers that I contacted for interviews were in the middle of production and on a distant location. Everyone checked their time zone and then pitched in and responded with warm enthusiasm and kindness. My friend, film historian Alberto Farina and his wonderful wife Chiara, interviewed, transcribed and translated my questions for Maurizio Millenotti and interfaced with him in Rome. I am grateful for all of their invaluable assistance.

My thanks go to the tenacious Elinor Actipis, formerly at Elsevier USA, who connected me to Mike Goodridge, the *FilmCraft* series editor.

After years of hounding Focal Press for a new edition of their costume design book, Ilex Press and Adam Juniper, the Associate Publisher, came to the rescue. Ilex's Managing Editor Natalia Price-Cabrera worked tirelessly on this volume to get it to press in record time and had a baby at the same time! Zara Larcombe and Tara Gallagher worked closely with all the designers to retrieve their text and personal images, coordinating my choices with Copley Center Assistant Natasha Rubin and with Kobal/Picture Desk to secure the stills for this beautiful volume. Costume designers will swear that we are "only as good as our team." Our credit may say, "Costume Designer," but our work always represents the contribution of an army of talented people. Without their support we would never be able to do our job. The same is true about this book, my title as author and editor, and the volume of writing and research that is produced from my office. My creative contribution is buttressed by my school, the UCLA School of Theater, Film and Television and Dean Teri Schwartz, my department and Theater Chair Michael Hackett, Alan Armstrong, my friend and generous patron David Copley, my graduate students, Daniella Cartun, Hannah Greene, Traci LaDue, Jaqueline Martinez, and Caitlin Talmage, and loyal alumni, Leighton Bowers, the "real" professionals Dorian Hannaway and Brenda Royce Posada, and my husband and enthusiastic promoter, John Landis. I would still be on page one if not for my brilliant assistant Natasha Rubin who juggles my projects like a Michelin-star sous chef. Natasha has coordinated the research, the sketches, and the text for three 2012 volumes, supported my 2012 Hollywood Costume exhibition at the Victoria and Albert Museum in London, and simultaneously managed the David C. Copley Center for the Study of Costume Design at UCLA. It is because of Natasha, John and my great crew that my name appears on the title page.

"If the designer can make the audience feel the actress is the character, then it's a good job of costuming." (Edith Head, eight-time Academy Award-winning costume designer.)

Deborah Nadoolman Landis
London, 2012

Jenny Beavan

"My process begins with breaking down the script on sheets of paper. Then I go through the script until I know it by heart and have lived and breathed each of the characters."

Through her 15-year collaboration with producer Ismail Merchant and director James Ivory, British designer Jenny Beavan earned early recognition as one of the premier designers of period costume dramas. Training at the Central Saint Martins College of Art and Design in London under designer Ralph Koltai helped Beavan secure a career as a costume designer for theater and opera. In 1975, Beavan began as an assistant designer on Merchant Ivory Productions' **Autobiography of a Princess** (1975). She went on to design costumes for the legendary Dame Peggy Ashcroft in **Hullabaloo Over Georgie and Bonnie's Pictures** (1978), and assisted costume designer Judy Moorcroft on Henry James' **The Europeans** (1979).

Throughout the 1980s Beavan continued to design low-budget, beautifully produced features for Merchant Ivory. In 1984, she teamed up for the first time with costume designer John Bright, owner and founder of the London costume house Cosprop. Their first film as co-designers, **The Bostonians** (1984), earned them an Academy Award nomination. Their inspired romantic designs for the Edwardian drama, **A Room with a View** (1985), won them the Academy Award and the BAFTA. This talented pair co-designed ten films, including **Howards End** (1992), **The Remains of the Day** (1993), and **Sense and Sensibility** (1995), and received a total of six Academy Award nominations and four BAFTA nominations.

Beavan is celebrated for her ability to create the past vividly. Her Oscar-nominated designs for **Gosford Park** (2001) and **The King's Speech** (2010) reveal the life and manners upstairs and downstairs. Whether designing for a 4th-century BC king in **Alexander** (2004), or a turn-of-the-century sleuth in Guy Ritchie's **Sherlock Holmes** (2009), her clothes and her "people" always feel truthful.

Jenny Beavan

" Both my parents were classical musicians who played with the Philharmonia Orchestra in London, my father a cellist and my mother a viola player. She gave up playing regularly to look after my sister Hilly and me. We were brought up in the middle of Kensington with very little money but a huge amount of music and interest in the arts, and we were always encouraged to draw and paint, and to make things at home. When I was three, my mother sent me to a dance class where I met a boy named Nick Young who came from a very rich, very generous family. Nick and his sister Sarah took Hilly and me skiing, horse riding and skating—all the things we couldn't afford under normal circumstances. My grandfather loved Shakespeare and used to give us sixpence if we could remember quotes, which was a lot of money in the 1950s. When I was ten, he took me to see Dorothy Tutin in **Twelfth Night** at the Old Vic. It was at that moment I knew that I had to do something in theater. My mother died when I was about 14 and a wonderful aunt and her two children moved in with us. We became a family of artistic children; my sister is a graphic designer and Rod works with wood. Clare went the scientific route; she's an osteopath.

In the 1960s, I played truant from school at little semi-professional opera and middle theater companies, stage-managing and painting scenery, and making tea. Somehow, I scraped together a couple of A Levels and went on to attend the Central School of Art and Design (now Central St. Martin's), where I studied stage design with Ralph Koltai. Ralph was known for his architectural vision of the set and was at the peak of his own design career. I loved conceiving and designing the space and Ralph told me that I was good at it. By the time I left the Central in 1974, I'd done some major design in the theater.

As it happened, Nick Young was helping on a film for Merchant Ivory Productions and drew me in to design extra bits and pieces. When Nick became Associate Producer of **Hullabaloo Over Georgie and Bonnie's Pictures** (1978) for British TV, Merchant Ivory needed someone to put together some clothes for Peggy Ashcroft and they called me. No money was involved, of course, but I was young and eager. Peggy played a mad English art curator in India and together we concocted a wardrobe from her old clothes, my old clothes, and bits and bobs. At our second meeting, Peggy asked me to come with her to India, offering to change her first-class ticket for two economy-class tickets. I did and I ended up

01–02 Jefferson in Paris

03–04 A Room with a View

looking after Peggy, helping with the props and the costumes and persuading coach loads of tourists to become background action in big scenes. That was how I became part of the producer Ismail Merchant and director James Ivory production family.

On their next film, **The Europeans** (1979), Ismail Merchant told Judy Moorcroft, the costume designer, that I would be her assistant. Suddenly, and without a clue, I was catapulted into that world of costuming. Before we left for New England, Judy took me to Cosprop; that was my first real experience watching someone develop costumes for a film and witnessing how a costume house works. The owner, John Bright, a designer himself, was fantastically supportive. It was all done in a much smaller way then and there were only the three of us working on the film. John and I became close friends and I consider him my mentor as well as my constant collaborator.

When Judy was unavailable to design Merchant Ivory's next film, **Jane Austen in Manhattan** (1980), my career was launched. Even though Ralph Koltai had taught me that costumes were "insignificant" I found that I quite liked costuming. The film is a fictional story and was based upon a lost manuscript of Jane Austen's that two theater groups vie to make into a play and opera, one traditional and the other a modern version. Jane Austen was shot in Manhattan and I brought a few costumes from England but mainly found them in New York. In those days, we took photographs of the clothes to show the director, and as I recall there was only one costume that I showed James Ivory that he →

didn't like. After **Jane Austen in Manhattan** I was considered a seasoned designer because of my relationship with Nick Young and Merchant Ivory, and I was hired to design contemporary drama and all 12 Gilbert and Sullivan light operas for British TV.

Soon I was back in the States with Merchant Ivory for **The Bostonians** (1984) and the following year we did **A Room with a View** (1985) in Italy and England. The budget was low but not impossible, and John Bright subsidized the costumes at Cosprop without question. James Ivory would wander up and down the racks with me to look at period costumes or I'd have clothes ready on stands for his review. We talked about colors. James wanted the Italian scenes to be fairly black and white and that seemed completely right; we followed the black-and-white or sepia-and-white historical photographs of the time. This was before the internet, and there was a great level of trust in my research. Since that time I've worked mostly as a period costume designer.

My process begins with breaking down the script on sheets of paper. Then I go through the script until I know it by heart and have lived and breathed each of the characters. The film I'm designing now is contemporary with a crowd scene at the Savoy Hotel, so I hang around the Savoy and watch who goes in and out of the lobby. I'm a people watcher. For **Alexander** (2004), I looked at vases in the British Museum; for **Sherlock Holmes** (2009), it was a mixture of old photographs and artists like Leslie Ward and Gustave Doré. Ward's pseudonym was "Spy"; he did fantastic caricatures of 1880s men wearing things you'd never dream of. The seamy, slimy side of London in Doré's etchings also seemed appropriate for these films. Then I trail around fabric stores because I need to get out of the house and away from the research to look at and to feel some fabric.

Every piece of clothing and armor in **Alexander** was designed and created because it didn't exist anywhere. Most of what we needed for the 19th-century **Sherlock Holmes** and for

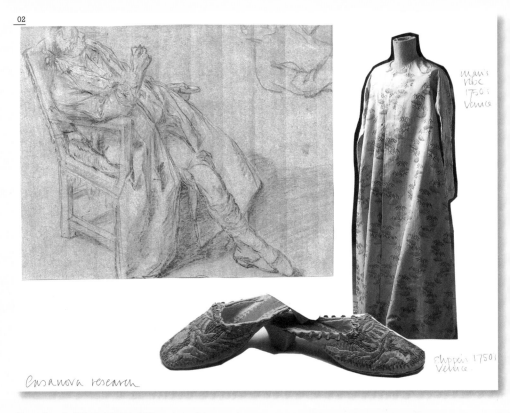

Cranford research

Cranford (BBC, 2007–09) existed in costume houses. I put together a notebook to remind myself of the different clothes that might be suitable for each character. I'll do a mood board but I don't draw, because drawing is two-dimensional and people are three. Only

01–02 Beavan designed the costumes for Lasse Hallström's **Casanova** (2005)

Working on a small budget

(03–04) "**The King's Speech** was a challenging film to design on a relatively small budget. The actors looked nothing like the 'real' people so it was a question of finding the spirit of each character rather than attempting a slavish depiction. We had about a minute to prepare the 'montage' sequence."

by putting the clothes on the actor do I really know what's going to happen; I've got much better at second-guessing, but sometimes a costume I think is absolutely right looks terrible. Now I dress up the stand, draping fabric and making prototypes; my cutter-fitter Jamie Law, or John Bright, do toiles [muslin prototypes] and we work on shapes and ideas until the whole thing comes together organically. By the time I get the actors, which these days is normally rather late, I'm pretty clear about which direction I'll go, and hope that I'm right. I welcome directors in the fitting room; then we're all sure that the costume is going to be right when it appears on the set.

Everything starts from the script and the director's vision. Some directors are happy that they've hired you and let you get on with it. There are directors who are control freaks and want to see every stage of the design and need choices and options. In the early days, producers hired me because of what I could do and directors loved what I did. Nowadays, I sometimes feel like a stylist, always showing options and bringing in clothes in every color. Younger directors want to make their mark and I've never worried about making my mark. I don't want to put "Jenny Beavan" on the costumes, I want to make costumes that are completely right on a particular actor, playing a particular part for a particular script. Costumes should support the actor's performance. →

05 The Remains of the Day
starring Anthony Hopkins and
Emma Thompson

SHERLOCK HOLMES

(01–03) "It's been a privilege to be a part of this new Guy Ritchie interpretation of the Sherlock Holmes stories and to create a 'new look' for Holmes and Watson. I love the way they use what I give them; clothes become part of the story when they borrow (or appropriate) each other's clothes."

01–02 Fabric swatches and visual reference material used by Jenny during the design process

03 Guy Ritchie on set with Robert Downey Jr. and Jude Law (respectively Holmes and Watson)

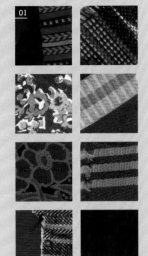

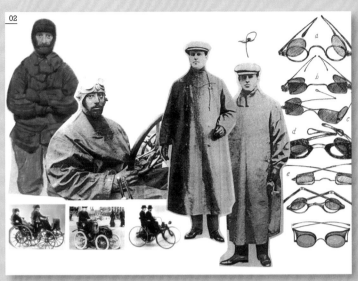

Costume design has far more to do with storytelling than to do with clothes. Fashion is the polar opposite of costume design because fashion is all about the clothes. Models on catwalks all look the same; it's their clothes that make them different. My job is about creating the person who's wearing the clothes. I always start from the character. Friends have told me, "I bet Jenny Beavan designed that film," then they've looked at the credits and there I was. That's not what I believe design is about, but if I do have some kind of style that people notice, I hope its "appropriateness."

Fortunately I've worked with brilliant actors. Judi Dench becomes whomever she's playing. Helena Bonham Carter would arrive for each fitting of **The King's Speech** (2010) straight off the **Harry Potter** set with one of the moustaches or beards and bits of her character "Bellatrix Lestrange" still attached. We'd have a cup of tea and put the 1930s' clothes on her and she transformed into the Queen Mum before my eyes. For **Sherlock Holmes**, Robert Downey Jr. adopts clothes and has lots of opinions and I try to add something of my own; it's very collaborative. Jude Law is lovely; I think of him as having a slight build but he becomes quite solid as Watson. The very thick tweeds of his three-piece suit give him weight without bulking him up.

As soon as possible I try to meet with the production designer and the cameraman to see if there are color schemes to consider, or if we're shooting in a spot where I have to worry about blue and red. Normally the three of us work as a team. The Art Department sends me fabric and color swatches or little storyboards. I've often worked with Luciana Arrighi and I adore her. Sarah Greenwood, the production designer on the **Sherlock Holmes** series is amazing. At the moment I'm designing **Gambit** (2012) with Stuart Craig, who designed Harry Potter. **Gambit** is a contemporary comedy and the director, Michael Hoffman, wants it to be really stylish. Except for Cameron Diaz, who's wearing real bling and trash, we're giving it a sort of weird elegance.

Tom Hooper, the director of **The King's Speech**, also liked to intellectualize; he'd talk at the ceiling about the characters and I thought at the time, "You can talk as much as you like, but we're not going to know whether we've got the spirit of these people until we put the clothes on their bodies." When he started to see what I could do, he realized how the character's relationship with costumes can work. Costume design must have an organic spontaneity about it; a designer has to have a bit of courage and just know when it works and then go with it.

In the end, costume design is whatever ends up on screen; it doesn't matter if the costumes were bought, designed and made, are the actor's own clothes, or something from the bottom of the closet. Collaboration and team spirit are essential. A lot of people deserve credit for a costume because it's always about other people's ideas as well as our own. As the designer, I guide and orchestrate the design of the costume. Actors think only about their character but I must see the entire story and the shape of the film.

My most challenging film was **Alexander** (2004). I took over the project from another designer who had done a lot of sketches but hadn't produced a costume. I knew nothing about Alexander the Great, and frankly I didn't know if he was Greek or Roman. I started my research from scratch with only 11 weeks before we packed and shipped the clothes for shooting. "I can do this," I thought, and rang my friend Stephen to come run the workroom. The next day I told him, "We can't do this in eleven weeks, even though the costumes are very simple." Stephen turned to me and said, "We'll do it in bite-sized chunks." That was the most marvelous and brilliant bit of advice. There are thousands of costumes in **Alexander** and I designed and we made almost everything. I didn't by any means get it all "right" but I'm really proud of leading a team that managed to achieve that huge film in record time.

To name my favorite film is tricky. It's between **The King's Speech**, **Gosford Park** (2001) and an HBO television film called **The Gathering Storm** (2002) with Albert Finney as Winston Churchill. I'm proud to have been part of these three →

GOSFORD PARK

(01–02) "We only had one vintage 1930s' evening frock for Mabel (Claudie Blakely) (02) in a 'tricky color green' as ad-libbed by Maggie Smith. It had to survive ten weeks of filming. The poor frock was glued together daily by Stephen Miles, a genius tailor, who only just forgave me."

DEFIANCE

(03) "We started with two jackets for Daniel, both made at Cosprop, and then realized we needed at least six in total. The very clever tailors in Lithuania copied it four times, but there were some very dodgy doubles due to not being able to find the same leather."

productions because of their visual and dramatic completeness. **The King's Speech** was tortuous for many reasons but each project ended as a happy experience.

The basics of costume designing haven't changed during my career but the circumstances have changed. Budgets are smaller and I'm often paid less now than I was at the beginning of my career. I certainly have less money to play with and less time to produce the costumes, which is hard on any movie. With all the new technology, producers and directors think that they can change their minds at the last minute, scripts change far more and productions are much more chaotic. Designers may have a bigger staff, but we need them with less time to produce the same number of costumes. The new technology also has enormous benefits: the fact that I can now do research online is brilliant. But the art of costume design hasn't changed at all.

The number one quality that a costume designer must have is a collaborative spirit. A designer absolutely cannot be grand, certainly not to do the kind of films that I design. And a designer needs stamina—the job requires such ridiculous hours and expectations. I look forward to going to work in the morning and seeing my team and then the bigger team on the set. It's the most marvelous, challenging, exciting, innovative job and there's always something new and wonderful to think about; I never have a chance to get bored. I rather love it when they say, "Jenny, have you got…?" and I think, "Bloody hell! No, I haven't…but maybe I can?" I love that kind of thinking on my feet. Designing is the only job that I know and I'll continue to do it until nobody asks me anymore, at which point I'll probably become a gardener.

Yvonne Blake

"From the time that I was a little girl I never wanted to do anything else other than costume design; I was always drawing brides, high-heeled shoes, and pretty clothes."

A gifted artist, Yvonne Blake studied painting and sculpture from an early age, attending the Regional College of Art in Manchester, England, as a teenager. At 18, Blake was hired as costume designer Cynthia Tingey's assistant at Bermans. Unfazed by the medieval period, she became the youngest member of the union when she designed the massive **Richard the Lionheart** (1962) for British television. Incredibly, her first feature film as a costume designer was Daniel Mann's moving **Judith** (1966), starring Sophia Loren, which she followed with two films for director Daniel Petrie: **The Spy with a Cold Nose** (1966), and **The Idol** (1966).

Blake won an Academy Award (with Antonio Castillo) for her hundreds of period costumes for the lavish epic **Nicholas and Alexandra** (1971), which portrayed the fall of the Romanovs. Her next two impressive projects, the Broadway musical hit **Jesus Christ Superstar** (1973) and Richard Lester's **The Three Musketeers** (1973), each earned her BAFTA nominations. Blake designed the luxurious costumes for seven of Lester's films, including **The Four Musketeers: Milady's Revenge** (1974), for which she was nominated for an Academy Award, the classic **Superman: The Movie** (1978) and **Superman II** (1980), establishing the super-hero film genre, and **Robin and Marian** (1976), starring Sean Connery and Audrey Hepburn.

Blake continues a distinguished career in costume design with the fantasy **What Dreams May Come** (1998), Milos Forman's **Goya's Ghosts** (2006), and the Spanish Civil War drama **There Be Dragons** (2011). She has designed many Spanish language films, working with such notable directors as Vicente Aranda, Ramón Fernández, José Luis Garci, and Gonzalo Suárez, for whom she has designed four films.

Yvonne Blake

My parents were both students when they went to England from Germany in 1936 to improve their English. My mother planned to be a foreign correspondent and my father was going to be a dentist. Hitler was in power and times were bad in Germany, so they stayed, got married and became naturalized as British citizens in 1947. During and just after the war, German immigrants in England had to do menial work. My mother worked as a court dressmaker in London, where they used to make the coronation robes. I was born just outside Manchester and grew up speaking English and German.

From the time that I was a little girl I never wanted to do anything else other than costume design; I was always drawing brides, high-heeled shoes, and pretty clothes. As I grew older my mother used to take me to the theater, plays and ballet at the opera house in Manchester and was always very encouraging. When she got my reports at school, art was always top of the list, although I was bad at most other subjects. "You find that with artistic children," the teacher told my mother, who was shocked. "Artistic?" she said. The school I went to was very progressive for the time, and encouraged students in the subjects that they were good at and completely neglected your weak spots.

At about the age of 12, I went to see **Funny Face** (1957, costumes designed by Edith Head, Paris "fashions" designed by Hubert de Givenchy), starring Audrey Hepburn and Fred Astaire, with wonderful clothes by Givenchy. That's when I decided I wanted to design costumes and I never faltered from that point forward. At 16, I was accepted into the Regional College of Art in Manchester to study painting, sculpture and fashion design. The other students in my group were much older than I was; they were all smoking pot and drinking beer, and I was still a little girl. But I was really serious about working and setting a career course. While I was there, I wrote a letter to Sally Jay, the set and costume designer at the Manchester Library Theatre Company, saying I was at art school and that I would like to meet with her. At that age I was a pushy little bugger, and she did hire me at 30 shillings a week to help out in the evenings. The repertory changed every month; we did plays from Arthur Miller to Shakespeare to Thornton Wilder. The London Festival Ballet used to come to Manchester to perform and their artistic director, Ben Toff, offered, "If you ever

ROBIN AND MARIAN

(01–02) "The costume that I designed for Richard Harris (King Richard) **(01)** consisted of a fur-lined embroidered long woolen tabard over a suit of "real" metal chainmail. It weighed a ton and he had to ride his horse wearing it. The costume was made at Bermans to his measurements, as I couldn't see him prior to shooting for a fitting. When he arrived for his only fitting on the set I couldn't even lift the costume. However, he walked straight into it, liked the way he looked in the mirror, and climbed up on his horse, using a stepladder. Looking at the film again recently, I wish that it didn't look quite so 'clean.' I didn't distress costumes as much as I do now."

come to London, see me and maybe we'll give you a job painting scenery."

When I was 17, I thought I wasn't learning much in art school, so I took my portfolio to London and stayed with friends of my parents. The husband made shirts for Bermans, the costume house, and arranged for me to meet the owner, Max Berman. He took one look at my sketches and asked what I wanted to do. When I said, "I want to be a costume designer," he introduced me to Cynthia Tingey. In 1957, most British films had somebody to do sketches and to design clothes for the stars, but they didn't always employ a costume designer to be on the set, as we do now. The costume houses in Britain had resident costume designers and Cynthia was Bermans' in-house designer.

Cynthia taught me about textures and fabrics and how costumes are made. She always painted with gouache colors on Canson paper and I've been doing that for the last 50 years, although we have completely different styles of drawing. I learned a lot from Cynthia. When the Brighton Ice Show needed a designer and Cynthia didn't want to do it, she gave me the job. All the big designers came into Bermans and just being in the same room, being at their fittings and holding the pins was a complete education for me. Working as one of Cecil Beaton's helpers on **My Fair Lady** on stage at Covent Garden, I was just so lucky, and I was like a sponge. I knew what I wanted to do and I was always very ambitious and very hardworking.

While I was at Bermans, Ben Toff introduced me to people at Royal Festival Hall and at the ballet, where I began to work. Through Ben, I also got to know Brian Taylor who offered me a job designing a television series. But before I started the job they had to get me into the union. When I asked how he'd do it Brian said that he would tell them that I was the only designer who knew enough about historical costume. That was how I became the youngest union member at 21. The series, **Richard the Lionheart** (1962–63), was pulled entirely from costume stock. I designed and made very few clothes because we shot two half-hour episodes a week—there simply wasn't enough time.

I've been incredibly lucky about being in the right place at the right time. After the television series I had a meeting with Basil Keyes. I knew that he was making a film in Israel, where I was going on holiday to visit family and he said to look him up when I got there. Basil was the →

GOYA'S GHOSTS

(01–03) "When I designed **Goya's Ghosts**, of course, Goya's paintings were my reference so the colors are much more subtle and the entire film looks much more believable, much more real."

01–02 Blake's original sketch with fabric swatches for Inês' (played by Natalie Portman) costume, and a still from the film showing how it was translated onto the big screen in **Goya's Ghosts**

> **"If the film has been well designed the audience shouldn't notice the costumes, unless it's the kind of film where the costumes were designed to look extraordinary and to be noticed."**

production manager on the film **Judith** (1966), starring Sophia Loren and directed by Daniel Mann. I ended up being the costume designer, apart from some of Sophia Loren's elegant clothes that actually came from Rome. I designed all the clothes that Sophia wore from the *kibbutz* laundry and I did have one or two things made for her in Israel. And I designed all the forties-era suits for the men. It was my first big film.

The most exciting part of a movie is the research and the meetings with the director. I like to work with interesting directors and I have worked with quite a few. Until I start designing I don't know exactly how I'm going to handle the project and as a result I'm not very good at job interviews where I have to sell my ideas. When a designer has a good track record, directors know that they can trust you. If possible, I prefer to repeat with directors; it gives me the confidence to make mistakes, even if later I'm told, "That's not the way I thought it would be." I like to take risks; I don't like doing the sure thing. When I am designing a movie, I always try to do something different, to put some element of surprise into the costumes and perhaps give them a sense of humor or add a period detail that I found doing research in the Prado Museum.

Before I put anything on paper I choose fabrics. For me, handling fabrics, feeling the textures and seeing the colors is more inspiring than looking at people's pictures. I have a very big collection of books of fabrics and I get swatches sent to me from Milan, Rome, London, and Frankfurt. Next, I staple the fabrics to a blank sheet of drawing paper, to see them all together and to plot the color scheme. Only then do I design the costumes. If it's a period film, I may be inspired by paintings; for **The Three Musketeers** (1973) it was the paintings of Van Dyke and Rubens. The designs for **What Dreams May Come** (1998), which was a fantasy, more or less came out of the back of my head, my imagination.

First I draw proper designs and then paint them with fabrics. If it looks good to me on paper, then the design will work. I really labor over what I do; it's like giving birth. I spend most of my time

rubbing out and changing things. I rarely hire a sketch artist because I find it very hard to explain to somebody what I want them to do. It's almost impossible if I don't draw the costume myself, because for me it all happens on the paper.

My most challenging assignment was **Jesus Christ Superstar** (1973), because Norman Jewison wasn't sure of what he wanted. The only clue that he gave me was, "These are kids doing a rock opera." "Should they look as though they made the costumes themselves?" I asked. He didn't know. So I drew lots of sketches and Norman would come to my studio and look at them hanging on the wall and say, "Yeah, yeah," which didn't help; I was having sleepless nights. Suddenly I saw the light: the design needed to be completely modern (1970s) with a biblical look. That was a tough film to design, but it's also one of the films that I'm most satisfied with; and when I see it now, it doesn't look dated.

Goya's Ghosts is one of my favorite films that I've designed. Another is **There Be Dragons** (2011), which goes through different periods and doesn't look "costume-y" at all. A lot of scenes occur during the Spanish Civil War, and what interested me was doing a film with realistic war sequences because I felt that the war movies I'd seen never looked real. I discussed this with Roland Joffé, the director, and convinced him that we needed to show all the shit and the blood and the gore. And we did, which makes the war scenes in **There Be Dragons** look really believable. Whether the film is contemporary or a period piece, as a designer I show the fashion of the time in which the film is set. Fashion is what people wear in any given time. The design reveals the social standing of the person I'm dressing; this is a statement of that time and in sociological terms. I think it's very important that costumes look like they're lived in, they mustn't look like they're fancy dress costumes. It's important that costumes are aged properly and then worn in the right way. Good taste and imagination are very important.

If the film has been well designed the audience shouldn't notice the costumes, unless →

it's the kind of film where the costumes were designed to look extraordinary and to be noticed. A long time ago I designed a film called **Green Ice** (1981) where the critics hated the film but they loved the frocks. That's not the kind of praise a designer wants. There's so much a designer needs to get right with a character to convince an audience. The actor has to feel comfortable in the costume and the costume has to look as though it's part of the actor to enable them to embody the role being played.

I was hired on the first **Superman** (1978) because I had worked with the producers on **The Three Musketeers** (1973) and **The Four Musketeers** (1974). Superman's costume was very problematic because he had to fly and we didn't have digital work back then. Superman was flying on a gimbal arm in front of blue and green screens. My goal was to design costumes like nothing seen before on screen. I got in touch with a factory where they made materials for

traffic signs that were reflective. Marlon Brando's costume was actually more of an idea from the director of photography, using this 3M material that they used to make cinema screens because of its reflective qualities.

This was early in pre-production, while they were still looking for an actor to play Superman, so there was a lot of time to do tests and come up with a final idea of how to design the costumes. We did masses of tests for fabrics and colors, and finally we came up with Lycra for Superman's costume. Lycra was a new fabric then and Superman's costume was one of the first Lycra designs to be seen in a movie. Our Lycra came from Austria and was specially dyed for us; I had the costumes made at Bermans.

During the screen tests for Superman, I was there for Christopher Reeve's test and he was so much better than anybody that they'd tested before. They'd even tested a Beverly Hills dentist for the part, dark and very good-looking, who, →

THE THREE MUSKETEERS

(02–04) "It was a wonderful experience to work with Richard Lester who has a brilliant sense of humor and a great visual sense as well. Each musketeer wore black and their collars and cuffs were created with fine guipure laces, and each of their costumes had its own special character. D'Artagnan (Michael York) was the youngest and most dashing member of the group, Aramis (Richard Chamberlain) was priestly, Porthos (Frank Finlay) was portly, and Athos (Oliver Reed) was a soldier and fighter. When I told our very elegant French costume supervisor that these costumes had to be very distressed and that all their lace must be ripped and dirtied, he blatantly refused. He was fired."

03–04 Blake's sketch for the costume worn by Milady (played by Faye Dunaway) brought to life in the still of the bedroom scene

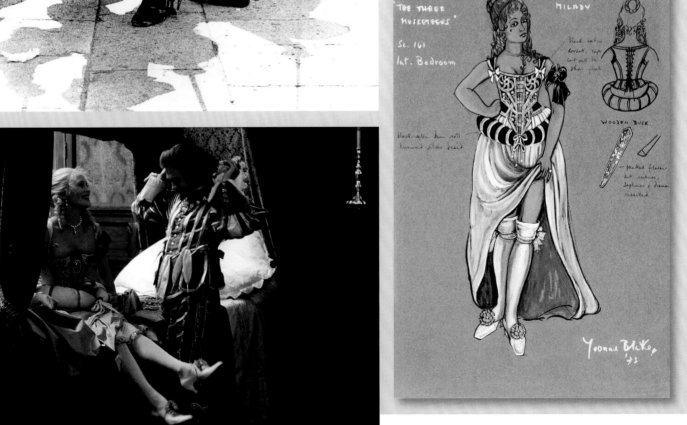

Superman'

Marlon Brando
as Jor-el.

Sc. Int. Council of Elders.
- trial of Jor-el.

Yvonne Blake
'76.

STOREHOUSE & DEPOSITORY

of course, couldn't act. And then we had problems with the suit because Christopher Reeve was nervous and perspired profusely, producing big patches of sweat. He tried all the different antiperspirants and the few that worked gave him a rash. So during the action sequences when he got wet under the arms we'd dry his armpits with hairdryers.

We made about 20 suits for him with different capes all in the same color but different weights. One cape was wool crepe, another was something more silky, and we switched them around depending on how they were used. We had a mechanized cape with a motor underneath on the shoulders for when we needed the cape to fly behind Superman. Another fabric was used if the cape had to wave in the breeze. It was all difficult, tricky stuff that is so easy to do now with digital work.

I've designed about 55 films and I've been working for more than 50 years. I always work at home unless my office at the studio is very isolated. And even then I make my office like home, very cozy with a sofa and the kettle and music. I like to work at night because

the telephone doesn't ring and I need full concentration because designing takes a lot out of me. My husband is a Spaniard and we live in Spain and these days that's where I work, but the work in each country for a costume designer is the same, I don't feel any different on a set in England, Spain or Hollywood, because a film is a film. Films are made in the same way and the process is identical. I think the more you do, the better you get; your eye becomes more attuned to more detail and you see more. But I do like the Spanish crews. They're very artistic. In the States I feel that it's all just considered an "industry," whereas in Europe I feel that it's an "art." That's the difference. 99

01–02 Marlon Brando's costume as Jor-El in **Superman: The Movie**

03 Superman: The Movie

The importance of original color reference material

(04) "Unfortunately, the sets and costumes for another film I designed at that time, **Nicholas and Alexandra** (1971, co-designed with Antonio Castillo), do look dated now. There was a big difference between designing **Nicholas and Alexandra** then and designing **Goya's Ghosts** (2006) 35 years later. A lot of research was needed on both films, but the photographs our big design team had for **Nicholas and Alexandra** were all in black and white. We used lots of bright blues and oranges, and colors that now look dated although they were rather daring in the 1970s."

NICHOLAS AND ALEXANDRA

(04) "A very somber scene of the Russian royal family waiting patiently to be deported, but sadly they were executed by a Bolshevik firing squad instead. The princesses were all dressed in gray flannel suits. The Tzar and his son Alexei were in typical Russian uniforms, and the Tzarina was very stoic in dark gray heavy wool crepe. Their costumes were based on historical photographic research of that time. Needless to say that when we shot this scene, the whole crew wept! The story of this family was deeply moving and while reading through all the research material, I was very often brought to tears."

05–06 What Dreams May Come.
The designs for this fantasy film were generated by Blake's imagination

Mark Bridges

"The most indispensable quality a costume designer needs is patience. Designers have to be patient at every point, at first with the producers and the budget, then with the actors and their schedules or idiosyncrasies. And…with the time it takes to build a costume."

Growing up with the long winters of Niagara Falls, New York, Mark Bridges became an avid film buff in grade school going to see old movies at revival houses. He attended Stony Brook University as a theater major, but spent much of his time in the costume shop. Determined to become a designer he landed a position at the preeminent New York costume house, Barbara Matera, before receiving his MFA in Costume Design from Tisch School of the Arts at NYU. His first film job was as a PA for Colleen Atwood on **Married to the Mob** (1988). Following that, designer Richard Hornung hired Bridges as his assistant on the Coen brothers' period tale **Miller's Crossing** (1990). Bridges relocated to Los Angeles to continue as Hornung's assistant designer on eight additional films.

In 1995, Bridges was introduced to writer-director Paul Thomas Anderson. Since then, these two artists have enjoyed a rich and productive creative collaboration; Bridges has designed the detail-driven and memorable costumes for all of Anderson's feature films, including **Hard Eight** (1996), **Boogie Nights** (1997), **Magnolia** (1999), **Punch-Drunk Love** (2002), and **There Will Be Blood** (2007). **The Master** (2012) is their sixth collaboration and at the time of writing is in post-production. Bridges' ability to bring eccentric characters to life has made him the go-to designer for edgy and authentic films. In addition to Anderson, Bridges has collaborated with director David O. Russell on the existential comedy **I Heart Huckabees** (2004), and the biopic **The Fighter** (2010), and with Curtis Hanson on **8 Mile** (2002), F. Gary Gray on the **The Italian Job** (2003), and Noah Baumbach on **Greenberg** (2010). His designs for Michel Hazanavicius' period film, **The Artist** (2011), brought him back to his childhood love, silent movies.

Mark Bridges

"Growing up in Niagara Falls, New York, winters were long and hard, and I had a lot of time to indulge in books of drawings and be immersed into the fantasy of movies on television. In elementary school I found R. Turner Wilcox's book *The Mode in Costume*, a historical survey with pictures, which fascinated me, without knowing why. My friends and I produced little stage plays, like silent movie melodramas. In high school, I became part of the drama club, which is a haven for a lot of kids. I was always into the movies and still have book reports from seventh grade that I wrote on silent movie stars. Two TV variety shows that I loved were **The Carol Burnett Show** and **The Sonny & Cher Show**, which were both designed by Bob Mackie. If I was aware that there was such a thing as a costume designer, it was because of Bob Mackie.

As a theater major at Stony Brook University on Long Island, I was acting and studying dramaturgy and writing. My hangout was the costume shop where my attitude was, "I'm going to be a costume designer." "We'll see about that," the teacher said. She was a designer and former member of the Costume Designers Guild, Sigrid Insull. Campbell Baird, who was my professor at Stony Brook, got me involved in an off-off Broadway production in New York of **The Stray Dog Story**, my first paying job.

By the time I graduated from Stony Brook I'd left acting far behind. Costume design had everything that interests me—history, shape, fabric, fashion, movies, drawing—everything that was natural to me. A month after I moved to New York I was working at Barbara Matera's costume shop as a shopper; the woman in charge knew Campbell Baird from when he'd mentored her husband. My job required me to learn my way around the notions and fabric shops, to find sources of materials. The old guard of costume design veterans used Matera's, fascinating people like Florence Klotz and Irene Sharaff. Matera's workroom also attracted the new guard of great designers—Milena Canonero, Julie Weiss, Willa Kim, Raoul Pene Du Bois—and also the emerging designers who would subsequently be big in the field, bridging both film and theater, like Richard Hornung, who was assisting production designer Santo Loquasto, and Shay Cunliffe, who was designing her first movie, **Mrs. Soffel** (1984). Every day was a new, exciting experience because I was learning so much.

During that time, I realized that I wanted to pursue costume design to the next level. Campbell Baird helped me get into the New York University MFA design program from which he graduated. At NYU my design professors were Fred Voelpel and Carrie Robbins, and the wonderfully eccentric John Conklin taught the history of art and costume. I got a sense of the historic chronology of dress and learned draping and clothing construction at a professional level. And I also learned that to work as a costume designer you need to deliver a costume on time in a disciplined manner and to leave no stone unturned in creating the best costume you can design.

Many of my NYU costume design peers decided to stay in the theater or wanted to

01 Brittany Murphy and Eminem in **8 Mile**

"None of us works in a vacuum. As a designer,
I serve the actors, the script, the director…"

design for opera and dance, but I always wanted to work in film. My first job was as an assistant designer to Carrie Robbins on **In the Spirit** (1990). Then, I helped out on **Miller's Crossing** (1990), sizing 1920s' clothes for costume designer Richard Hornung. After that, Richard asked me to come to Los Angeles to assist him on **The Grifters** (1990). We worked out of Richard's apartment, using tear sheets from contemporary magazines for inspiration. For each character, for each change, we'd do a hairstyle, a length of skirt, the shape of a shoe and an accessory sheet. Richard and I and another assistant spent two weeks (a luxury of time that we really don't have any more) collecting more tear sheets, doing research, and copying, cutting, pasting and putting them all together in a design presentation. We got the look of the movie and the characters down cold—the shape of every shoe, watch, the jewelry, everything.

Sometime after **The Grifters**, I was recommended to John Lyons, who was →

03 Uma Therman as Edie Athens in **Be Cool**

BLOW

(02) "This ensemble seemed right for this moment when George is in Miami and very cocksure of himself after selling a great deal of cocaine. He doesn't know that he is about to be taken to Columbia. The inappropriateness of the outfit adds to the sense of abduction while communicating that George is someone special. It was very difficult to schedule time with Johnny Depp. I had gotten his sizes and we had two brief meetings. I went on pulling a variety of interesting clothes in vintage stores and unsold goods from the period in the basements of stores in downtown LA. It all came down to fitting Johnny the night before filming. Together, we went through the 30-year arc of George's character in three or four hours. I refined and refit him daily as he established the 40 plus changes that he wore in the film."

01 Bridges' concept boards for different stages in Dirk Diggler's career path for **Boogie Nights**

02–04 Bridges' costume designs as seen in the film

05 Breakdown showing the different color palettes used during different periods in the film

1977	Seq "A"	1978 Seq "B"	1979	1980	1982 Seq "C"	1983	1983 Seq "D" march	1983 sept	Seq "E"	1984 June
1	55	76	83	87	96	112	119	151	188	195
70's COLORS	LET THE GOOD TIMES ROLL RAINBOW COLORS			ACID TRIP WIERD COLORS & GLITTER	BEIGELAND		DIRTY LAUNDRY			COLORFUL NOTE
					end "C" 106					
54	75	82	end "B" 86	95	December 111	118	end "D" 149	Dec-83 157	end "E" 194	

BOOGIE NIGHTS BREAKDOWN

A personal favorite

(01–05) **Boogie Nights** is one of Bridges' favorite films to have worked on. He saw it as an incredible job to be involved in and a great platform to show what he could do. Of this movie he says: "**Boogie Nights** was a labor of love. Going to work every day was exciting because I love that period of the 1970s. We were all young and enthusiastic; there were great actors on the project and the story was really fun. It was very well received and I was very proud of the movie."

producing a film for first-time director Paul Thomas Anderson. Paul and I met at a restaurant in the San Fernando Valley and I took him to a screening of **The Investigator** (1994), a small period film that I'd designed for Chanticleer Films. He liked what I'd done with the story and hired me to design his first movie, **Hard Eight** (1996). I'm currently designing my sixth movie with Paul; we've been working together for 16 years now. Paul likes to work with the same people, but it's hard to schedule because he works only once every four or five years. There's a real family vibe when we all work together. That doesn't mean it's without its occasional tensions, but there is understanding and the collaboration is there; you're not going to get that the first time working together.

The most indispensable quality a costume designer needs is patience. Designers have to be patient at every point, at first with the producers and the budget, then with the actors and their schedules or idiosyncrasies. And finally, a designer has to be patient with the time it takes to build a costume, and patient with your co-workers. If you don't have patience, you're constantly frustrated and the tension bleeds into all the other areas. I don't know if I am always successful, but I am learning that patience is necessary.

None of us works in a vacuum. As a designer, I serve the actors, the script, the director, and the director of photography. My ideal experience is a back-and-forth with the director with some tempering and guidance. I respect their vision and they respect mine; we all have the same goal. I avoid jobs where the designer has to send pictures of what they are planning for each character off to some mysterious entity (like the studio) for critique. My attitude is that either they don't need me (if they're going to pick the clothes), or "If that's what you want, I'll get it, but I can't take responsibility." Luckily, this kind of creative intrusion hasn't happened recently, but I have had experiences where producer interference was shocking.

Whenever possible, I do my own primary research. Even though costume prep time on

movies is truncated now, I still follow Richard Hornung's process of preparing a research bible so that everybody knows what I'm doing. Mostly I do tear sheets, even when I'm designing a period film, then mood sheets or specific images that give the vibe of each scene, whether I have the exact garment or not. Often, that's enough to convince the director I'm going in the right direction with the design of the story. Then, he'll see pictures from the fittings showing what the →

01 Nicole Kidman in **Fur: An Imaginary Portrait of Diane Arbus**

THE FIGHTER

(02–04) "It was a challenge to create a believable, accessible character yet keep the essence of Alice Ward's personal style, which I felt spoke volumes about who she thought she was and wanted to be. The HBO documentary **High On Crack Street** (1995) provided great research and showed that very specific time in Lowell, Massachusetts. The 'real' Alice Ward presented herself as a combination of sexy and tough, coordinated and accessorized. Ultimately, she was a force of nature in animal prints and plaids, with the bag always matching the shoes. First, I adjusted Melissa Leo's silhouette with body shapers. Then, I went searching for unusual designs from the late 1980s and early 1990s; period prints, shoulder pads, nipped waists, body suits and slim skirts. Combining those elements with Melissa's new blond hairstyle was very exciting (02). I knew that we were successful when 'Alice' materialized about halfway through that fitting."

03 Christian Bale and Mark Wahlberg in **The Fighter**

04 The Ward sisters in the film showing the fashion of the period

costumes are really supposed to look like. I refer to this research book all the time. That's really important.

If it's a period piece, I review what research may work for the film, asking myself what piece of clothing is right for the character. I love to put my hands on clothing, to really delve into the research, and to look at contemporary photographs and films, but I'm not big on creating my own costume drawings. With a contemporary screenplay, I try to figure out who the characters are and what style of garments they would wear, where they would shop, how they feel about themselves. Their shoes, the way they wear their pants, will speak volumes to the audience. After I've distilled each look, I start to shop for the character or copy something that I find in my travels. If I'm designing a look that's edgier or trendier, I'll go to Japanese fashion magazines to see what's coming next in fashion; that strategy has served me really well in the past. Then, I'll mix a jacket of one suit with a different style of pants and then create it all in one fabric. The creative path I take depends on the character and is specific on a case-by-case basis. If I need to, I'll design all the pieces, but I don't have to make everything for every movie. You're not going to find the right fabric, or be able to afford to make the clothes, or have the time to make them on every film.

I arrive on a picture maybe two or three weeks later than the production designer. The length of the prep doesn't affect me negatively, but the amount of time I have with the actors does. I wish that the production could settle on casting the actors sooner. It takes at least two fittings to get the actor ready for the camera. The first pass for the design is a "meet and greet" where we talk about the character and I check out their body type. The next step is to figure out what will work for the actor, the hem length, the shoe height, their hair coloring, everything. I share my ideas, we discuss the colors, and afterward I rethink the costume precisely for the actor I am dressing. Whether the design works or not is another challenge; I'm so interested in what actors are

01 Adam Sandler as Barry Egan in **Punch-Drunk Love**

doing and to hear where they are coming from. They're all so different and cool in their own way and how they approach a character.

Being on the same page with the production designer is so important. Designers that I admire most take an idea, run with it and make their own world. I try to check in with the art department and ask, "Is there anything I need to know?" It helps the storytelling if we can talk about wall colors and I'll give them some ideas that I'm going to do, my palette, because that helps the storytelling. And I'll run ideas by the production designer, but we're usually not working in the same place. He's location scouting, and I'm away, so we check in with one another, but we're not sitting in the same room plotting each shot. There are some technical components of filmmaking that I may not be privy to, a certain lens, or the director and the DP will talk about processing the film in a certain way. Sometimes I get left out of those conversations. It helps to try to run ideas by the director of photography, to be deeply involved in the camera tests and dailies, and to gather as much information as possible.

My Hollywood career has been spent trying not to get pigeonholed as the designer of one genre. At this point I've created a large body of work that could be known, for lack of a better term, as my style. It looks real, it looks offhand, →

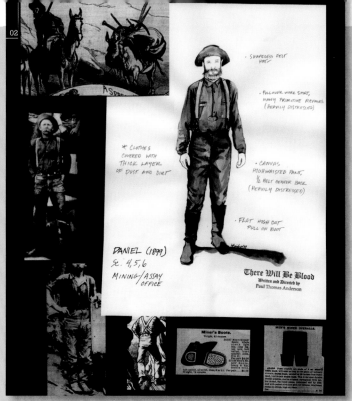

THERE WILL BE BLOOD

(02–03) "Daniel's suit was one of my few luxuries on the film as I was able to have the fabric custom-woven for this suit, and both the suit and shirt were custom-made. His iconic hat was rented from a costume house and his tie was purchased from a vintage dealer. Young 'HW' had a rented period shirt and an antique suit that needed many repairs during the rugged shooting schedule. None of this seemed to have bothered Daniel Day Lewis who loved the energy and well-worn patina of the clothes, and made them an integral part of his character. He commented on the vintage oil drilling gear that he tried on at his first fitting saying, 'I'd do this film just to be able to wear this costume.'"

it's got a lot of texture, and hopefully it doesn't feel super-designed. Consider **8 Mile** (2002), **There Will Be Blood** (2007), **The Fighter** (2010)—everything's up there on screen so that you understand who these people are and become involved with the story. Unfortunately, I don't know if the costumes looking "real" and not "designed" is a good thing for the costume designer. But designer Theoni Aldredge always said, "If they don't notice the clothes, you're doing your job."

The personal favorites of my films are **Boogie Nights** (1997) and **Blow** (2001). On **Blow**, director Ted Demme was a wonderful mellow guy who allowed me to do my thing. One time, Ted asked me to take a hat off an actor, but otherwise, whatever the actors wore to the set Ted put on film.

My most challenging film was **There Will Be Blood**, which was shot in a remote area in West Texas. Paul Thomas Anderson found a 60,000-acre ranch and the production designer, Jack Fisk, built a little train station, a little town, a church on the hill, an oilfield and a farm. There weren't even roads until we arrived. We were night shooting on a Thursday when Paul informed me, "We're going to reshoot on Tuesday with a

new concept." "Excuse me?" I said. We didn't have the period clothes and there was no such thing as overnight shipping to this remote Texas location. The airport was a three-hour drive away. On Friday morning, I called for help in LA and told them what I needed. On Tuesday morning I dressed the actors. Somehow, I did it, but I wouldn't like to do it again.

People have asked me, "Would you ever want to get into fashion?" Costume design is based on characters in a script with a certain arc within a story and we are trying to support that story. Costume is one element of a dramatic presentation. To me, costume design has nothing to do with commerce or bringing attention back to the designer, whereas fashion designers have their own publicists. Fashion is about commerce first—then art. I like to think that costume design is about art—then commerce. Ultimately, a fashion designer's goal is to make something people want to buy and costumes are just one part of a movie. It's not my goal for people to want to buy what I've designed.

Since my career began I've seen a big change in the costume workplace. When I started out, I designed my own smaller budget independent films between the union films that I was assistant-

01–02 Bridges' costume sketches for the film and Ben Stiller as Roger Greenberg in **Greenberg**

designing for Richard Hornung. For three or four years I worked with a really small straight-to-video company that produced a lot of sci-fi and kids' movies. I could design films in town, switch over to be the costume supervisor on an HBO movie and then assist designer Ruth Myers on a video. Now those positions are split between two different union locals; the costume department has been segmented. It is much more difficult to go back and forth the way I used to.

For designers today, there is less money, less time, less staff and more unrealistic expectations from the production company about what can be accomplished. All these constraints on our resources make it harder to produce something good, and it's an uphill climb for costume designers. As to where the movie business is going, recently at Cannes, **The Artist** (2011), the black-and-white silent movie that I designed for French director Michel Hazanavicius, was very well received. Maybe that's not a novelty. Maybe the industry can get back to basics and forsake some of this computer-generated 3D craziness that seems to be happening right now? Maybe, we'll get back to telling stories. **"**

03–05 Bridges' sketches for the characters George and Peppy, and a still from Michel Hazanavicius' 2011 film, **The Artist**

Danilo Donati

"He liked my shirt," Donati recalled of the first time he met Federico Fellini. "It was actually a dreadful shirt, but we became friends." Born in 1926 in Suzzara, Italy, Danilo Donati studied fresco painting at the Academy of Fine Arts in Florence. He had planned to be a painter, but began his artistic career as director Luchino Visconti's costume designer for large theatrical productions. His film career began in the 1950s for directing legends Roberto Rossellini and Pier Paolo Pasolini. In 1967, his work on two films **The Gospel According to St. Matthew** and **La Mandragola** garnered Academy Award nominations. A year later, Donati won his first Oscar for his work on Zeffirelli's memorable **Romeo and Juliet** (1968). But it was his 20-year collaboration with Fellini that would define his career.

Fellini, who once described Donati as, "A great connoisseur of art in the body of a variety show dresser," was already a well-known director by the time they collaborated on **Fellini Satyricon** (1969). The pair discussed the movie for a month before Donati felt ready to design for the maestro, as Donati remembered, "Fellini told me to do whatever I wanted, but I understood from the first day he needed something timeless and unreal. The fundamental thing was to destroy any references to factory-produced clothing. I made a basic form to suit everybody, changing the materials and colors, yet still allowing the faces of the characters to remain the dominant factor.

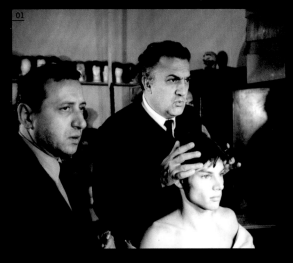

01 Danilo Donati on the set of **Fellini Satyricon** with Fellini and Harim Keller

02 Flash Gordon

03

04

05

"Fellini once described Donati as 'A great connoisseur of art in the body of a variety show dresser.'"

The great challenge was to remove everything, leaving only the metaphysical." During pre-production Donati described Fellini as "very intelligent, open to any experience or experiment."

Once the film started production, however, their relationship became turbulent. The script proved only to be a springboard for the director, and was never adhered to, as Donati shared: "There has never been a practical discussion with him and the script doesn't serve any purpose. You have to prepare only for what is needed in each scene." He described the experience of working with Fellini as, "like walking on the edge of a knife blade." Donati was constantly exasperated by Fellini's methods of working, "You must never listen to Federico, only interpret. If you listen to him, you only arrive at madness. Interpreting him is the only way to be close to him."

Despite the overwhelming experience, the pair, who Fellini described as due fratellini

(two brothers), continued to work together. On **Roma** (1972), Fellini asked Donati to take on the additional responsibility of production designer. Though he "absolutely didn't want to design the sets," Donati was grateful for the experience explaining, "Fellini discovered a potential force in me which I held inert, and gave me the courage to confront it." In all, Donati designed seven movies for Fellini, including the highly regarded **Amarcord** (1973), and Fellini's **Casanova** (1976) for which Donati won his second Oscar.

Donati continued to work as both costume and production designer throughout his career, including the cult classic **Flash Gordon** (1980) and two films for director Roberto Benigni: **Life is Beautiful** (1997) and **Pinocchio** (2002). Benigni reminisced, "I was convinced Danilo Donati was immortal. I was so used to seeing him seated in his chair like a demigod. He dedicated his life to the service of beauty. All the world will be forever be grateful to him." Donati passed away in 2001.

03 Fellini Satyricon

04 Casanova

05 Romeo and Juliet

Shay Cunliffe

"A designer must be flexible and not lose her head when important things are being decided and changed in the moment. It also helps if you can put your ego in a bag by the door."

Shay Cunliffe went to boarding school in England at age 11 and graduated from the University of Bristol with honors. Moving to New York in her 20s, she worked at the New York Review of Books, and then became director Mike Nichols' assistant. She took classes from the Art Students League and enrolled in Lester Polakov's Studio and Forum of Stage Design. With enhanced confidence she started at Barbara Matera Costumes where she assisted the legendary Irene Sharaff on a revival of **West Side Story**. After assisting Julie Weiss on a Broadway show, Julie recommended her for her first film, **Mrs. Soffel** (1984), starring Diane Keaton.

Cunliffe designed three more films starring the discriminating Keaton, including **The Family Stone** (2005). She collaborated on three films with independent director John Sayles, including the critically lauded and elegantly rendered Texas border town saga, **Lone Star** (1996), **Of Mice and Men** (1992) for actor-director Gary Sinise, the James L. Brooks films **Spanglish** (2004) and **How Do You Know** (2010), and Ken Kwapis' romantic comedy hit, **He's Just Not That Into You** (2009) and his upcoming **Big Miracle** (2012).

Cunliffe's diverse repertoire includes the dramatic films **My Sister's Keeper** (2009) and **A Civil Action** (1998), the horror films **The Believers** (1987) and **Dolores Claiborne** (1995), blockbuster action films in which the costumes must disappear, such as **The Bourne Ultimatum** (2007) and **2012** (2009), and the animated feature, **The Simpsons Movie** (2007), on which Cunliffe served as a character costume design consultant. Cunliffe's signature includes a talent for mixing costume metaphors, great taste, and an easy versatility through genre. She is currently designing **Django Unchained** for Quentin Tarantino (2012) starring Leonardo DiCaprio and Jamie Foxx.

Shay Cunliffe

" In 1956 my mother, Mitzi Cunliffe, designed the golden theatrical mask, now recognized as the BAFTA (British Academy of Film and Television Arts) Award. My father was a professor of American history and literature at The University of Manchester in northern England, but he was finishing graduate work at Yale when he met my mother at a party in New York in 1949; she was the gorgeous young queen of the art scene. Six months later she moved with him to Manchester, where I was born. My father, being a historian, and my mother, an artist who adored clothes, provided the two strands in making me who I am—a professional costume designer. Every other year my father taught in American universities and the British schools that I attended were much more advanced than those in the United States. When I was living in the US I was the class genius, and when I returned to Manchester a year later I'd be so far behind in my studies that I needed remedial help until we were off to the States again and the cycle repeated itself. It was then that I learned that you're neither the best nor the worst in anything—it's all context.

During my teens I attended school in London and spent every lunchtime in the costume and textiles section of the Victoria and Albert Museum; week nights I'd buy five-shilling tickets to the Royal Shakespeare Company and the Royal Court Theatre. Very early on, I knew that my passions lay in costuming and the theater. During the political 1970s I studied drama and French at the University of Bristol. After my parents divorced, I helped my mother move back to America in the mid 1970s and decided to stay two years to see what developed. In those days I went to job interviews in old overalls, a Victorian top and ballet slippers with ribbons tied up my calves and was repeatedly reprimanded by the job agencies. What's interesting is that once I became a designer my personal dress habits became less eccentric.

I delivered a Driveaway car to San Francisco and once there I cleaned houses and handed out fliers on street corners. I got very stressful phone calls from my mother saying things like, "Will you please do something normal and real. Get a grip, it's time." I got a phone call out of the blue from someone in the editor's office at *The New York*

Review of Books that Robert Silvers needed an assistant. "Would I want the job?" I didn't have the money to get out of San Francisco, but my mother said, "What on earth are you talking about? I'll lend you the money to get a plane ticket."

My first day of work, before I even put my handbag down, they said, "You've got to get V.S. Naipaul on the phone because his piece is late." Susan Sontag came in later that afternoon, she was sitting on my desk wanting to know what galleys had come in that were interesting. Everyone in New York would come and hang out. *The New York Review of Books* was somewhere that I didn't have to wear high heels and I could wear my ballet shoes. And I credit myself with getting the bluestocking women of New York to loosen up. The wonderful satirical writer, Prudence Crowther, was the typesetter at the time and she started dressing in more eccentric ways. She said, "You know, you've given smart woman permission to wear lipstick and wear ridiculous dresses to work."

A man who was friends with one of the editors was setting up an office with Mike Nichols. He said, "Mike Nichols needs an assistant and he can't bear people who can't write proper letters. Do you want to come and meet him? We'll pay you twice as much." I had loved **Catch-22** (1970), but I didn't know anything about the famous Elaine May and Mike Nichols act, and in fact, I didn't really know the place that Mike Nichols held in American society. I remember going for the interview in the most unglamorous outfit (hiking boots, a long tweed skirt and a mismatched Fair Isle vest and cardigan) just in case there were any misunderstandings about the sort of assistant I was going to be.

Working with Mike Nichols I met a lot of theater people including Nancy Potts, the costume designer. When I told her that I loved costume design, but didn't pursue it because I couldn't draw, she responded that drawing could be learned. That was maybe the most →

01 John Cusack in 2012

02–04 Cunliffe's sketch and original inspiration for the Tibetan grandmother's costume, and how this translated to 2012

"For a while I felt that I didn't have the necessary drive to go into film design, but after battling for jobs every three months I realized that life is a battle and you don't have to be a warrior to fight it."

important thing anyone ever said to me, though it took six months to percolate.

After a holiday in England I returned to New York feeling very depressed. I wrote to Nancy Potts who suggested that I go to The Art Students League on weekends and take night classes at the Lester Polakov Studio & Forum of Stage Design. "Go there and do the script breakdown class, the drawing class and the design class," Potts advised me, "and when you start working in the field don't get stuck in the workroom in the back, be a shopper. You'll meet all the designers and learn all the resources you'll need to know."

Six months later, I designed a show at St. Clement's Episcopal Church for a fee of $50 and a budget of $150. With not much experience under my belt I thought, "Okay, I'll tackle it." A few months later I decided to make the leap and luckily, set and costume designer Tony Walton, whom I'd met through Mike Nichols, offered to call Barbara Matera Costumes for me. In 1979, a few days after I started at Matera, Irene Sharaff came in to discuss the **West Side Story** revival. She'd come out of retirement and had no assistant and Matera was very, very busy. I was assigned to

assist her and at the time I didn't realize how incredible that was. My job was to swatch her fabrics and escort Ms. Sharaff, who was very frail, out every night and get her into a cab.

For a while I felt that I didn't have the necessary drive to go into film design, but after battling for jobs every three months I realized that life is a battle and you don't have to be a warrior to fight it. Barbara Matera had recommended me to Julie Weiss, who then called me to ask for help on a small Broadway play while she was also designing a movie. Julie then recommended me for my first film, **Mrs. Soffel** (1984), assisting Luciana Arrighi, who was also the production designer. I didn't realize at the time that I was going to be the costume designer until Luciana told me to get all the costume stock together and to start sourcing makers for all of Diane Keaton's and Mel Gibson's costumes. Then she left for England to do the production designs.

My process begins by reading the script several times and then meeting very quickly with the director to learn the kind of film he's planning to make. I put together the research, padding it out visually and researching the world in which this

02 Reese Witherspoon and Owen Wilson in **How Do You Know**

DOLORES CLAIBORNE

(01) "Kathy Bates played Dolores Claiborne, a woman who was much younger and then much older than Kathy at the time of filming. This is the younger Dolores—a 'flashback' from her happier past. For this change, I designed an old-fashioned maid's uniform with a light color collar to frame her face and a golden floral print apron to convey a sweet and cheerful innocence. In contrast, the older Dolores wore dreary, formless clothes and no longer bothered wearing a uniform at work. The boundary between her and her employer had broken down over the years, which is reflected in her informal clothes."

story is going to take place. For a contemporary story about firemen, it means that I have to go to the firehouse and talk to them, have the firemen put on their work clothes and explain to me how they function, showing me every detail. I may even want to put the clothes on myself to see how they feel. My research consists of putting all the visuals, the photographs, Xeroxes, and the notes together to share with each new member of the team, including the actors. I'm intuitive and perhaps feel my way into a production more than some other designers.

For contemporary films it's more about making mood boards; I tend to sketch only when I know that I'm making a costume. I don't like to sketch if it's not something that is going to go into production because so many things can change between the sketch and the fitting room. I made that mistake early on in a contemporary play. I sketched out the characters and then I couldn't quite find what I had sketched. I'd rather we started from a real place; there's something about custom-made clothing that feels too perfect. That's fantastic for a slightly otherworldly quality or wealthy characters, but the designer risks losing the underlying realism of the piece with custom-made clothes.

At the first fitting I would much rather try real clothes on the actor—even when I'm going to make the costumes. I'm not going to make a →

HE'S JUST NOT THAT INTO YOU
(03) "Gigi (Ginnifer Goodwin) is the girl who tries too hard, including in her choice of outfits. She 'pulled together' this ruffled blouse and tan sweater vest to convey a bit of girly charm and a lot of poor fashion sense, which she wore on a blind date which didn't go well at all. Luckily, Ginnifer was a very enthusiastic collaborator and we had some wonderful fittings playing with racks of clothes to hit just the right misguided 'look' for Gigi. Ginnifer was delighted to play someone who loves clothes, but doesn't get it quite right."

decision from a sketch because so many shapes won't work. I'm going to also want to try prototypes of the costume in the fitting so we can all see how the fabric behaves. Actors stimulate me and I stimulate them. When actors give nothing back it's a dreadful few hours. I've shown costumes to a director and got it wrong, but the directors that I love are very nice about it. A few can be extremely rude and dismissive and throw a cloud over me, while I am trying to keep very clear-headed and upbeat, which is really important for my team.

A costume designer must be able to listen carefully. It's a huge asset to have my assistant in the fitting room to tell me, "I know you thought that the actor was agreeing, but I felt so much hesitation, I think that you should be open to that thought." There's no point trying to talk anyone into anything, later it will come round and bite you. Even if I believe my design is fabulous I always prepare another choice. But it's hard when I've spent an inordinate amount of my budget on that first choice and it's got to fit the stunt person too. I try and have a plan B and a plan C at all times. A designer must be flexible and not lose her head when important things are being decided and changed in the moment. It also helps if you can put your ego in a bag by the door.

01 Chris Cooper in **Lone Star**

WHAT A GIRL WANTS

(02) "This is Daphne Reynolds' (Amanda Bynes) ultimate fairy-tale moment, her 'coming out' ball in London escorted by her long-lost father (Colin Firth). This gown is one of the costliest garments I've ever had constructed, as I've had to tell the many girls who emailed me wanting a dress just like it. Neil Cunningham, a fabulous young couturier in London, made the gown of heavy ivory *peau-de-soie*. The look was inspired by Audrey Hepburn's magical elegance with a hint of a **My Fair Lady** transformation. Two identical gowns were ordered due to the potential damage over one week of energetic filming."

John Sayles is a fabulous director to work with because he trusts his designer and provides a huge amount of information about his characters. He writes a page of back story about every single character in his movies, even the bit parts. Each back story includes intimate information that is nowhere in his script, including their childhood, their dreams for themselves, their fears, and where they're heading in life; it's all there. John and I have worked together about four times and we hardly need to talk at this point.

Every film contains its own very hard element and sometimes it's just the job at hand. Ken Kwapis' **Big Miracle** (2012) recreates the 1988 rescue of whales in the Arctic Circle. The film opens with the whale hunt. I didn't know anything about that world and it was very hard getting the research. I ended up finding Inupiat Eskimos who could make the clothes, because I realized that this would really matter to the Inupiat Eskimos who were playing the parts.

Films used to have a couple of producers. Now, I can be emailing my fitting photos to eight different people without knowing the pecking order of whom I have to report to. They cast the actors on Sunday night, email the contract to the actor's agent, email me a fitting photo and put me in touch with the actor who's going to wear my costume tomorrow morning. But it takes me not one minute less time to source the right fabric, gather it together, figure the costume out in a fitting and have it made. It takes exactly as much time as it would have taken a designer putting on **Macbeth** in the 19th century.

I seem to be the go-to contemporary designer, but having designed quite a few period films, I love the moment when I've managed to successfully recreate another time. A director once remarked on my eclectic résumé. He said, ''When I look at your portfolio I see a very clear style. I see extremely simple, not fussy, a kind of cut-to-the-chase clarity about these costumes.'' I'm good at putting aside my own aesthetic likes and dislikes to serve the film and I hope each project has a successful life of its own. →

THE BOURNE ULTIMATUM
(03) "I distilled Bourne's (Matt Damon) 'look' down to one of pure, utilitarian simplicity. My goal was to create a totally functional and forgettable garment so that Bourne could move efficiently and invisibly through the world. Twenty-five copies of these jackets were needed to handle all the abuse they would take during the action sequences. I also needed to adjust the proportions of several jackets to suit specific stuntmen, and I created a series of increasingly 'distressed' jackets."

"I tend to sketch only when I know that I'm making a costume. I don't like to sketch if it's not something that is going to go into production because so many things can change."

The **Bourne Legacy** (2012) has one of the things that strikes terror in my heart as a designer: two lead characters who do not have many costume changes. There are about four beats, four different looks, and chase sequences where the man and woman do not change their clothes. Added to that, the characters are undercover in a world of anonymity—another tricky thing that is absolutely antithetical to the designer's task. Yet somehow I have to cheat the flatness of it all, to create in that anonymous context and still draw the eye of the viewer to the important points in a crowded scene. Because that's what costumes are meant to do: to flag

THE FAMILY STONE
(01) "Tom Bezucha, the director, had a strong visual idea to create a timeless quality using a tight color palette and no blue whatsoever. The family's costumes were designed with a warm palette that was full of pattern, texture and idiosyncratic personal touches. In contrast, Meredith's (Sarah Jessica Parker) alienation from the family group is reinforced visually with every outfit. She is rigid and constrained, and she cuts a darker, stylish silhouette in beautiful clothes."

Working your way up the ladder

(02–03) "My husband was a set designer and seeing me hysterical, he said, 'How hard can this be? You just need a costume breakdown sheet.' He drew boxes on a sheet of paper and said, 'Look, you write the script day, the costume, the character. What else?' Today, I still operate off Xeroxes of that same breakdown. It's primitive, but almost a talisman for me; I calm down when I see my breakdown sheet from 1983. I started at the bottom and worked my way up every little rung of the ladder with **Mrs. Soffel**. The film is set in 1899 and for the first time, I flew to LA and pulled period clothes out of all the studio costume departments. I forged a million new relationships and I learned that a designer is only as good as her team. After that, I was officially a costume designer."

moments, flag people, direct the viewer's attention to what's important. I'd much rather they needed 40 costume changes; this is like a tightrope.

Years ago I designed a film called **Blood In, Blood Out** (1993), about rival Latino gangs in East LA. As part of my research I met a lot of gang kids and realized they only wore three things. I invited about 40 of them to the costume department and we looked through racks and racks for different ways to vary the look. They declined to wear just about everything I put together, sullenly and shyly picking the same two things. Then, I had an epiphany: the gang wanted a uniform—that was the point; that was the design. It was probably obvious to anyone but a costume designer. In the end, a really good costume design is so at one with the story that even if it's a period film the audience isn't thinking of the clothes; the film is about the story and the characters. Sometimes I long to get a film that is about the clothes, but then I'd probably have to write it myself. ""

SWEET NOVEMBER
(04) "Sara Deever (Charlize Theron) was an irreverent, thrift-shopping 'Boho.' I had a great time pulling this character together in the thrift shops of San Francisco, checking out the places the character would shop as my foundation. Nearly all of Charlize's costume pieces came from eclectic sources since she and I felt that her character would also be very 'crafty.' Charlize's mother crocheted several pieces, such as the scarf in this picture, and her costumes were truly a 'homemade' effort."

Sharen Davis

"To design for film you have to see things through the camera; you can't trust your eye. Designers should take classes to learn the different kinds of film stock and lighting techniques that affect how the costumes will look on screen."

Born in Shreveport, Louisiana, to a military father, Sharen Davis grew up in Japan and Germany before returning to the US to study acting at the Pacific Conservatory of the Performing Arts. After a stint in the art department on a Roger Corman movie, Davis worked as a costume supervisor for seven years, including for the film **Mississippi Masala** (1991), starring Denzel Washington whom she knew from her theater days. She went on to design five films starring Washington, including director Carl Franklin's **Devil in a Blue Dress** (1995) and **Out of Time** (2003), and two directed by Washington, **Antwone Fisher** (2002) and **The Great Debaters** (2007).

Davis' talent for realizing an authentic character and her ability to gain the confidence of her actors can be traced back to her theater days. She is a treasured creative partner of movie stars Eddie Murphy in **Doctor Dolittle** (1998) and **The Nutty Professor II: The Klumps** (2000), and Will Smith in **The Pursuit of Happyness** (2006) and **Seven Pounds** (2008). She created over 100 elegant changes for Oscar-winning Jamie Foxx in **Ray** (2004), director Taylor Hackford's biopic of legendary soul singer Ray Charles. Her designs earned her an Academy Award nomination and high praise from the late singer's family. Sharen brought the Motown scene to life for the musical **Dreamgirls** (2006), starring Beyoncé Knowles, and illustrated the girl group's style evolution from the soulful early 1960s to the disco era. **Dreamgirls** earned Davis her second Academy Award nomination. Her most recent work includes the Hughes brothers' post-apocalyptic **The Book of Eli** (2010), starring Denzel Washington, and the wonderfully fresh, funny and sensitively designed film adaptation of Kathryn Stockett's bestselling novel, **The Help** (2011).

Sharen Davis

"Japanese and European fashions were among my earliest influences. My dad served in the US Air Force in Japan during my high school and college years and my mother and I shopped endlessly in Tokyo. In the 1970s, Japanese culture reflected an influx of European and American influences. When my family moved back to the US, this country represented a whole new world to me at 19. I was wearing styles that hadn't reached the States yet and people laughed at my maxis and platform shoes. I fell in love with films and went to the movies day and night. **Bonnie and Clyde** (1967) mesmerized me, and I saw **Annie Hall** (1977) ten times.

At that point in my life my mother still shopped for my clothing but I re-made everything, which infuriated her. That's where it started—I was a "closet designer." I put together outfits for my friends, telling them they should dress closer to their personalities. My father wanted me to join the military to be an officer, but I wasn't equipped for that, even though I had a high-grade point average. Instead I studied acting, first at the Pacific Conservatory of the Performing Arts in Santa Maria, California, and later at the American Conservatory Theater in San Francisco. Although I was a good singer and a good dancer, I was never a good actress, and eventually I lost interest in pursuing that career.

I moved to Los Angeles and was hired to work in the art department on **Galaxy of Terror** (1981), a Roger Corman production, and James Cameron was the production designer. It was like the art found me; I immediately fell in love with the way the camera sees the world and ended up taking night classes to learn about textures and colors. Costume designer Kathie Clark taught me how to break down the script when I assisted her on **Valet Girls** (1987), and how to be a costume supervisor. "Use your acting skills and push the clothes," she'd say. It was easy for me to talk to actors because of my acting training; I knew how to arc the emotions of a character using costumes, which is how I work to this day.

Tracy Tynan was one of the first designers I worked with. She was designing from LA so she couldn't go on location when we shot **Permanent Record** (1988) up in Portland. There was a

01 Alicia Silverstone, Golden Brooks, Queen Latifah, Sherry Shepherd and Alfre Woodard in **Beauty Shop**

> **"My acting skills have helped me as a designer; I begin by reading the script twice as the lead characters and going through their emotional arc."**

performance of **H.M.S. Pinafore** inside the film. It was pretty big for my third film. Because Tracy wasn't there it was a huge responsibility for me as a supervisor, and I wanted to make sure that I was doing exactly what she wanted to do. She was so clear. Tracy is so brilliant and way ahead of her time; she filmed fittings to see how the clothes moved on the actors. She always encouraged me and was a great role model; now I always have my fittings photographed.

I was a big fan of Alan Rudolph's, and it was exciting for my first film to be with the director of **Choose Me** (1984) and **Trouble in Mind** (1985), both designed by Tracy Tynan. I thought he was brilliant and such a visionary at the time. **Equinox** (1992) was a horror movie; Alan looked at me and said, "Monet. I want the whole palette to be Monet." And we're in Minneapolis, and, "I want a dual time period, 1920s and modern day. So have fun." **Equinox** is my favorite film because it was so creative and not contemporary. "This is what being a designer is," I thought.

My acting skills have helped me as a designer; I begin by reading the script twice as the lead

02

characters and going through their emotional arc. Then I visualize the set and the interaction between the characters and the extras. And I memorize the dialogue so I never have to look at the script when I talk to the director about characters and scenes. On a recent interview for a big period film with lots of twists and turns, the director was shocked that I understood the subtleties of the screenplay without explanation.

When I'm designing a period film I'm drawn to the Burbank Public Library. I have my own research at home, but I love to have the librarians pull books for me. Fabrics and textiles inspire me and I try to see how far I can go mixing periods to create more original designs. My current project, **Django Unchained** (2012), is about a freed slave who assists a German bounty hunter before the Civil War and could be set anywhere between 1830 and 1860. I made a notebook of the periods and used it as my visual presentation to the director, Quentin Tarantino. "There's a big arc," I told him, "and you might want to pick a year. Here are the possible looks." When Quentin interviewed me, he hadn't seen any of my work but he knew that I'd designed **Ray** (2004), which he didn't see. "I don't like biopics," he said. Before our second meeting he saw **Ray** and then couldn't stop talking about Jamie Foxx—who he then hired to star as Django! It was so funny.

My last fantasy film, **The Book of Eli** (2010), is set in a post-apocalyptic society but the director wanted me to use existing periods so I mixed them the way we wear clothes in real life. Today, you see people in 1980s-style clothes; they don't look like how we wore them back then but the silhouette's the same. There are great creative tailors and seamstresses in Los Angeles and I use more than one workshop for my films so there isn't just one hand making all the clothes. With different tailors, every character has a different cut and style. John Hills at Universal Studios Costume Shop and I work together often. Usually my films shoot in the South and I prep the clothes in Los Angeles and then bring one cutter/fitter with me on location. My assistant designer stays in LA to work with John Hills →

02 **The Great Debaters** directed by and starring Denzel Washington

DEVIL IN A BLUE DRESS

(01–02) "Denzel Washington portrays Easy Rawlins, a working-class man who gets involved in a mysterious woman's complicated world of criminals and politics. Rawlins' closet consisted of the basic essentials: one suit, two dress shirts, casual jacket, work jacket, four casual shirts, a pair of dress slacks, work trousers, dress and casual shoes, T-shirts, two hats and basic accessories. When Rawlins is out of his comfort zone, I had to re-invent this small closet. I wanted to be obvious about combining casual shirts with dress slacks and his one suit for church becomes a disguise for his everyday wear. I used his work jacket with a logo to move him through neighborhoods where Rawlins needs to be invisible. Rawlins in his comfort zone, maybe at a local bar, looks comfortable yet sexy."

01–02 Jennifer Beals and Denzel Washington in **Devil in a Blue Dress**

Dreamgirls
Ferrell, Effie and Deena
Costumes by Sharen Davis

and sends me illustrations and anything else I might need.

Rian Johnson's **Looper** (2012) takes place in 2030 and 2060 and he emphasized that he didn't want anything that looked like **Star Trek**. It's hard to explain fantasy design since it really comes out of your head. The challenge was to design something dismal without being drab— you can't take life away from human beings. My solution was to use hues of the same colors and no jewelry. In this future, people use hair and makeup to show their creativity and wealth, and the hair and makeup in **Looper** are wild. I felt honored that Rian picked me—he could have hired a younger, hipper, more stylist-type designer. But I did take issue with his vocabulary. When he said, ''You understand that I don't want the wardrobe to stick out,'' I responded, ''Do you mean costumes?'' I always ask when they use the word ''wardrobe.'' When the crew list comes out and says ''wardrobe department,'' I ask, ''What department is that?''

To design for film you have to see things through the camera; you can't trust your eye. Designers should take classes to learn the different kinds of film stock and lighting techniques that affect how the costumes will look on screen. Once I was watching dailies and thought, ''Wait a minute, that costume did not look like that.'' Then I realized I'd used 100-speed film for my fitting photos and the cinematographer was using a different stock. Now, I always ask the director of photography what stock they are using and I get the same film. On **The Help** (2011) I couldn't get anything approved by the production because they didn't understand that fitting photos are a work in progress. Then I had the production's professional still photographer, Dale Robinette, take the fitting photos and once Dale started shooting my costumes, everything got approved.

On **Looper**, I built my own costume design website for the director. That was a mistake because Rian Johnson looked at everything on his iPhone. There's no way to make costumes look great on a smart phone. Halfway through the production I went back to shooting the clothes on 35mm film, developing prints and bringing them to the set in a folder. The pictures were bigger and clearer. ''This is great!'' Rian said. ''It's so much better than on my iPhone.'' →

03 **Dreamgirls** illustration by Felipe Sanchez

04 The costumes as they appeared in the film of **Dreamgirls**

Turning a challenge into a success

(01–03) "My most challenging assignment was **Ray**, an independent film with no budget and action spanning from 1929 to 1970. Jamie Foxx had over 100 changes, and all his clothes were made to order. The director, Taylor Hackford, gave me one note: 'Use your creativity and wisdom to transform Jamie Foxx into Ray Charles. I don't want anyone to see Jamie in this movie, I want them to see Ray.' His trust in me was inspiring. Every morning I meditated to come up with a concept to make it work. All my energy went into Jamie because he's in every scene. I put his clothes in six closets that I created for each style change and we repeated a lot of his shirts. Ray Charles loved Nat King Cole and the 1950s' clothes reflected that elegance. With prosthetics over Jamie's eyes making him blind, I made sure he knew all his clothes by touch. The result was awesome—Jamie channeled Ray. But I didn't have one day off during the entire production."

He's young and didn't know this was old school, how we did it before computers. He thought it was a brand new idea.

In movies with African-Americans, white fabrics against dark skin is a big issue. Working with the production designer, I test at least ten variations to establish the standard white for clothes, sheets, apron, curtains, everything, because it really will not work on screen if all the whites are different. We try to use the same gray or tan tech [dye shade] throughout the film design. Because of this, I need the cinematographer to be my best friend. Philippe Rousselot is brilliant and knows how to bounce the white without resorting to tech [over-dying fabric]. When we were making **Antwone Fisher** (2002), Denzel Washington said, "Why would you 'dinge up' that wonderful white uniform?" So we did not tech those US Navy uniforms. Denzel, with his beautiful blue-black skin tone wore the white Navy uniform; it's stunning. Denzel and I met at ACT, before he became a big star. I've designed many films in which he starred, including the two movies that he directed.

Dreamgirls (2006) was hard because my style is to underplay the costumes and I felt like I was designing a fashion show, not characters in a movie. After **Dreamgirls** I designed smaller, independent films where I didn't have any pressure. I was horrified when I first saw the poster for **The Help**. "Oh, my God, I thought I underplayed it. Those dresses are so bright! Where's all the flowers and plaid? Did I do that?" I was panicking when I saw it! I thought I'd stayed true to what the author told me about the clothes when I first met her. The young girls from the South wouldn't look like sophisticated New York ladies. They dress up, but they look young, like little flowers. The film is set in 1964 in Mississippi, where domestics did wear white uniforms to clean houses; they still do. But in white uniforms the maids looked like nurses—we tested them and they looked weird. When my grandmother was a domestic in Louisiana, she wore gray, as most domestics do around the world. So I used gray and the studio agreed with me.

It's important to be aware of everyone's position on a film, to be positive and open to suggestions. J. Michael Riva was the production designer on **The Pursuit of Happyness** (2006) and **Seven Pounds** (2008), and now we're working together on **Django Unchained**. We discuss colors and try to subtly create a mood so that maybe no one (except us) will notice it. The hair stylist on **The Help** was Camille Friend, who I've worked with on four films. Sometimes the hairstyle does not go with the dress; you don't want a flip where it should be a chignon. I'll show Camille an illustration and say, "This is what I'm

thinking, what do you think?'' If she says, ''That's going to be impossible, I can't make her hair do that,'' I change the illustration to make it work for her and the actress.

Actors come into fittings with their entourages now, suggesting things, and producers also have a say. It's important not to argue, to let them say what they're going to say, but don't think you have to do it. It's all political skills and the first hurdle is getting people to trust you and to believe that you'll come in on budget. A designer has to take the studio and production manager from right brain to left brain. The clothes are secondary. Some bigger studios send you tear sheets and dictate the color of the clothes, they're into everybody's business. If it's a first-time director who doesn't know anything, the production designer and I really need to help him. Politics suck up valuable production time and leaves designers with five minutes to do their job.

Nowadays a designer has to work for weeks doing research without pay to get what they eventually want to see on camera. If you or your agent fights for more paid time in prep the production company will replace you with another designer. For **Django Unchained** I have nine weeks' prep. I told them that I would start three weeks early without pay but they had to pay the illustrator and my assistant. I don't care →

04 Chris Tucker and Jackie Chan in **Rush Hour**

01

02

03

04

05

06

about the extra prep because director Quentin Tarantino is a visionary and I know he's going to make a great film. I want to do my best work and if that means working extra weeks for free so that my designs will be right, that's my choice.

The future? I'd love to design a fantasy film like **The Lord of the Rings** (2001). I still sing, I need to do more of that, and I'm taking vocal lessons. And, I love to cook. After eating jambalaya my whole life, I created a recipe that is really good, using clean, organic ingredients. It took forever, but after five years I think that I have it down and I'm thinking of getting a storefront or a truck and selling it. Absolutely everyone loves it and friends often ask me to make it for parties. Shrimp or vegetarian—there are a million ways to make jambalaya and ten ways to serve it. **"**

07

THE PURSUIT OF HAPPYNESS

(07) "Chris (Will Smith) is picking up his son from daycare and trying to rush to the shelter to get a room for the evening. Chris floats between two worlds with only one look: the business world during the day and at night, a shelter. His closet includes three suits, five shirts, six ties, three vests, one Member's Only jacket, work jeans (from when he served in the Navy) and a pair of Top-Sider slip-on shoes that are all packed in one piece of luggage. His clothes are dated and worn, but Chris handles them with care. At first glance, his suits are acceptable, but when he is in a scene with a co-worker or called in a meeting with the Boss, we can detect the poor quality and the wear and tear that time has taken on his clothes."

01–03 Gina Flanagan's illustrations for costumes worn by several of the leading characters in **The Help**

04 & **06** Hilly and Celia, leading characters in the film, translated onto the big screen in **The Help**

05 The original color for the domestics' uniforms in **The Help** was white, but Sharen changed this to gray with the studio's backing

Lindy Hemming

"Ever since I have worked in theater I have developed an active desire to explain to people what costume designers do because I feel that we've been treated as secondary members of the whole process."

A self-proclaimed student of the human race, Lindy Hemming enjoyed little exposure to cinema in her rural Welsh town. She began a career as an orthopedic nurse before finding her way to the theater. After graduating with a degree in Stage Management from the Royal Academy of Dramatic Art in London, she spent the next 15 years designing costumes for Charles Marowitz's Open Space Theatre Company, the National Theatre, the Royal Shakespeare Company, and London's West End. Before her film career got started, Hemming was honored with a Tony Award in 1983 for **All's Well That Ends Well**.

At the National Theatre, Hemming met director Mike Leigh, who became a long-time creative collaborator, culminating in an Academy Award for her superb character study and sensational costume designs for **Topsy-Turvy** (1999). The great success of the trend-setting independent film **Four Weddings and a Funeral** (1994) earned her a BAFTA Award nomination and the attention of James Bond producer Barbara Broccoli. Hemming designed five Bond films, redefining the look of the British spy for Pierce Brosnan in **GoldenEye** (1995), and accomplishing that makeover again for Daniel Craig as Bond in **Casino Royale** (2006).

From the meager budgets of Channel 4 to the franchise action-adventure films **Lara Croft: Tomb Raider** (2001), **Harry Potter and the Chamber of Secrets** (2002), and **Clash of the Titans** (2010), Hemming is a true master of the medium with unparalleled experience. It was no surprise that she was the prominent designer chosen to collaborate with Christopher Nolan for his visionary retelling of the Batman story, the hugely successful trilogy: **Batman Begins** (2005), **The Dark Knight** (2008), and the upcoming **The Dark Knight Rises** (2012).

Lindy Hemming

"We lived in an old farmhouse on a mountain in Brechfa, Wales. My grandmother was quite artistically inclined. She was fortunate enough to be one of the only girls admitted to an art school in Sheffield in the 1900s. It was a guild craft school, because Sheffield was the home of silver and stainless steel. From the art school she was chosen to be a designer of such things as the Calcutta Cup (rugby union trophy), knives, forks, spoons, and teapots. My mother also had a craft bent; she used to make most of our clothes, and she made jewelry from seeds, butterfly's wings, and dried flowers. My father worked as a salesman and also did wood carving that he sold. We had no money. Everything that my parents crafted was taken to the local market in Carmarthenshire where they had a stall one Saturday a month. The whole family would go and my siblings and I would live under the table. I always watched people from below and examined what they were wearing and guessed who they were.

We moved to a village shop in Cryg y bar, which was more "grist for the mill" of observing people. If you live in the village shop, you know what people eat, what they smoke, what newspaper they read, and when the ladies have their periods; you know everything. It was a human parade and it was fantastic. If I have to attribute one thing to my career of designing costumes, it was the early adventure in human examination that was my childhood. I hardly saw any movies growing up because I lived in the middle of nowhere. I really was a theater person, not a movie person. I used to go to the Old Vic and see stuff like **The Royal Hunt of the Sun** and things, and then I started to feel "I wish I could do that." **A Man for All Seasons** (1966, costume designer Elizabeth Haffenden) was the first film I saw when I eventually moved to London, and then I started to think, "That's a real thing that somebody is doing! It's not just that I like doing it, it's something that people do, and there is a trajectory to this job!" →

01–02 Lindy's working drawings for the three Little Maids and Timothy Spall's character as The Mikado for the film **Topsy-Turvy**

01

02

The importance of the costumes beyond the film itself

(04–05) "Even though I had designed Bond, **Lara Croft: Tomb Raider** (2001) was my first real understanding of the world of super-heroes and designing films to make toys, DVDs, and games, which they then sell and make loads of money. By the time I designed **Lara Croft Tomb Raider: The Cradle of Life** (2003), I understood that the return isn't just what the studios make from the film, it's the money they make from all the other allied products. And I finally recognized the role of the costume designer as the designer of these toys and games. I grasped the power of product placement and how a designer can use it and work with it for the benefit of the picture."

TOPSY-TURVY

(01–03) "Working with director Mike Leigh for about 20 years makes one forget his unusual improvisational work process. It was the creative opportunity of my life to be asked to design **Topsy-Turvy**. I had the luxury of time to research all the aspects of both the principal characters and the period of the story while working with the actors playing the principal roles. I primarily used cheap fabrics and dyed, appliqued and painted them. The actors rehearsed in period corsets, footwear and clothing, and were actively involved in the design decisions as we proceeded. The stage production of **The Mikado** was designed and custom-made, as were most of the principal costumes."

> "At this grand old age it's really thrilling to work in a genre where I get the opportunity to design things using modern technology."

My father was a socialist who believed that you should give back to the community. He said that instead of going to art school, which is what I wanted to do, I had to do something "good." I became an orthopedic nurse, which, he imagined, would precede a life as a physiotherapist. While I was nursing, I met a young folk musician who worked in the hospital. We began a folk club together and eventually he went to the Royal Academy of Dramatic Art (RADA) in London. When we were saying goodbye he said that I should be a stage manager because I was so good at organizing. This was the very first time that I realized that I could have a career in the theater. Some months later, I went to London and applied for a place at RADA to learn stage management.

At RADA, the woman who interviewed me seemed to be in terrible pain. Instead of carrying on with the interview I said, "What's wrong with you? If you don't mind me asking?" and she said, "Nothing, really." I said, "But something's wrong." She was suffering from an awful slipped disc and I told her exactly what she should do for relief. The acceptance letter said, "You will be fantastic at dealing with actors. You may not yet know what that means, but you will. You have a place here at RADA." But by then I had found out that I was pregnant and could not take the place. I never told the school that I was pregnant or when I had my daughter, Alex. Finally, when she was eight months old, my grandmother (the designer) said, "You must take that place, you can't not take it, so few people get the offer. I'll look after Alex and you'll live with me." Within a very short time I went from nursing to being a mother, to being at RADA. Thanks to Grandma Harpenden.

When I got there, I had no concept whatsoever of what I was doing. There were stages, there were tutors, there were actors, and I'd never met an actor in my life. It was the period in modern British history when we poor bohemians were meeting middle-class and upper-middle-class people from privileged homes and we were all banged together in college along with kids that had come from Liverpool on grants. It was a very rich mixture of people. At the stage management course my sideline was designing the costumes and I understood immediately that design interested me. I took full advantage of Douglas and Jenny Heap, the tutors of the theater design and props course, and insinuated myself into the costume design workshop. On weekends I'd be with my daughter and then head back to school on Monday.

Director/critic/playwright Charles Marowitz, an American, had the very famous alternative off-Broadway Open Space Theatre in Tottenham Court Road. He was the first theater director who took me seriously and used me properly as a designer. It was mad working at the Open Space Theatre. We were buying clothes for a production of **Woyzeck** from army surplus and we got paid almost nothing, £200 for a production or something, but it was worth it. From there I moved to the Hampstead Theatre Club and worked for director Michael Rudman, a Jewish Texan who had come to Britain to go to university and ended up staying on and running this theater. Rudman talked about character and he went through the script with you in depth. I learned to do my job the way I wouldn't have learned it unless someone was interested in me personally. He remains one of the best directors that I've ever worked with in my life.

When Mike Leigh came to the Hampstead Theatre Club to direct **Abigail's Party**, it was the beginning of my understanding that the script and the character is king. In Mike's case, he invents it with the actor. You're not there to do your own thing; you're there to do what you can to enhance the character. Michael Rudman and Mike Leigh were the directors who gave me that insight. Director Alan Ayckbourn and I worked together at least eight times. Everything he has written is about how human beings behave and he is an observer of the human condition *par excellence*. As our shows started to move to the West End Michael Rudman took me with him. I like to work with one person and stay working with them. I don't care if my career would have gone faster or in a different direction if I had let →

01–03 Halle Berry as Jinx, with Rosamund Pyke and Ricky Yune in **Die Another Day** and Hemming's illustration depicting Jinx's "biker-type" suit worn in the film when she is in Iceland

DIE ANOTHER DAY

(01–03) "The orange bikini choice seems like a very simple one **(01)**, but many conversations and much deliberation went into the idea of revisiting the Ursula Andress bikini look from **Dr. No** (1962, costumes designed by Tessa Prendergast). In the script, Jinx (Halle Berry) is a hot tempestuous Cubana who has to appear to be a normal holidaymaker before the audience discovers her true intentions. This gave me the opportunity to dress her in bright colors that during her chase scenes and against the dark cliffs and emerging from the rather grey sea off Cadiz, would make her glow, catching the eye of Bond who was having a beer at a beach bar. This was also a rare situation in a film where the leading lady would really look great in these hot pinks and oranges. I approached the underwear and swimwear makers, La Perla, with my design ideas; I had worked with them before. I showed them my color reference and they made the simple, beautiful bikini in multiples. Next, I thought about how to update the knife belt. I looked at lots of modern diving belt reference and fashion belts and then designed a Bond girl version. I approached the leather workers Whitaker Malem to construct it in both a waterproof and non-waterproof version. Their finish is unparalleled and their design suggestions resulted in my stainless steel D-shaped buckle design turning into 'J' for Jinx!"

my ambition pull me away. It's been better for me to work with the same people and let them lead me. When Rudman was asked to run the Lyttelton Theatre at the National Theatre, I followed, and worked there for seven years.

The National Theatre had the most fantastic government-funded wardrobe department filled with tables of cutters, beaders and dyers, run by Ivan Alderman and Stephen Skaptason. When I walked in I had no idea how to manage what I was doing. I got all my information on "how to behave" from these costume people, who'd worked with Laurence Olivier. They used to say "Darling! Bea Dalton [costume designer Phyllis Dalton] wouldn't have done that." Followed by, "You're not going to a second-hand shop are you?" They were learning a kind of "street" thing from me and I was learning how to run a workroom from them. It was like going to the "university of costume." It only ended when the theater was taken over by biscuit factory managers who had to make it profitable. I did 15 years of theater and for ten years of it I was in and

out of the National, the West End, and the Royal Shakespeare Company.

When Channel 4 Films first started they were making small, low-budget films. We didn't have a lot of film directors in Britain except for the really famous ones, so they asked theater directors Richard Eyre and Mike Leigh, who I had worked with at the National. **Meantime** (1984) was the first film I designed for Mike Leigh and it was the first time that I understood how closely the camera looks at everything. I began to think of films as individual frames, including all the little nuances that you can put into characters in films that are lost on stage. Because of the way Mike Leigh directs, I attended the rehearsals and then costumed the actors while helping them bring their character to life. If they were to play a nurse, or an engineer, I would begin researching the characters with Mike and the actors. Often, I would go to watch those people at work because that is what Mike requires the actors to do. And because Mike requires the creative team to be in rehearsals and

FOUR WEDDINGS AND A FUNERAL

(01–03) "The idea was that Gareth's (Simon Callow) waistcoat **(03)** was a contribution to building his witty, clever, naughty, generous and prankish character, and that he was openly and happily living as a gay man. His clothes helped make him more likeable so that his sudden death would be all the more shocking and wasteful. Small character touches help the actor build and flesh out the character. I found the illustration of boy cherubs kissing in a book of Victorian engravings. I drew it up on a paper pattern of the waistcoat and when the fabric pieces were cut I asked an artist to paint it. The characters in **Four Weddings and a Funeral** were so well-written and well-observed of a certain class section of British society. In spite of the really tight budget I had a fantastic design and on-set team, and we begged and borrowed to costume the seemingly endless cast."

improvisations, we start on the production a long time before the film starts shooting.

For **Topsy-Turvy** (1999) I researched costume drawings and the biographical backgrounds of the real people [composer Sir Arthur Sullivan and librettist W. S. Gilbert] at the V&A. You can glean things like Gilbert liked to wear this color, or that Sullivan was rather grubby. The way Mike Leigh works meant that everything that we want to do as costume designers, I was given the opportunity to do properly. Instead of just being told to go and hire something, like "This person's just been cast and they've got to be Abraham Lincoln. Go and hire the costume." I could study the way they walked, their habits, the underwear they would have worn, and then construct it. The actors and I entered the rehearsal period with a lot of accurate information. Then, our actors had to rehearse in the corsets, with the canes, the top hats, and for actor Allan Corduner [Sir Arthur Sullivan], rehearse with the monocle.

As with **Topsy-Turvy** there was little budget,

but lots of pure invention in Peter Chelsom's **Funny Bones** (1995), which starred Oliver Platt, the comedian Lee Evans, Jerry Lewis, Leslie Caron, and Oliver Reed. Set in Las Vegas and Blackpool, it's a cult film about, "What is funny?" The eccentricity of the cast of characters, the Blackpool landladies and circus performers gave me the opportunity to design all kinds of lovely things. There was no budget, so I relied on pure invention. Later, I was designing a small film called **Sister My Sister** (1994) when I got a phone call from Tony [Anthony] Waye saying, "I'm ringing on behalf of [James Bond producer] Barbara Broccoli, they need to meet with you for the new Bond film, **GoldenEye** (1995)." I thought it was one of my friends having a joke. I asked, "Are you from Disney? Do you want me to design a new costume for Mickey Mouse?" I didn't know what they wanted me for; I couldn't understand. So they said, "We watched **The Krays** (1990) and **Four Weddings and a Funeral** (1994) and we think you're the right person to put a bit of new life into Bond." I said, "I think you've made a →

> "The one indispensable quality a costume designer must have is patience, because the things that we have to do are quite crazy most of the time."

mistake, but I'm really interested. Of course, I'd love to do it."

When I designed **Harry Potter and the Chamber of Secrets** (2002), Judianna Makovsky had already designed the first movie, so we maintained the original characters, but I particularly enjoyed designing the Weasleys, who were just starting off then. Michael O'Connor, my assistant designer, and I had great fun re-inventing witches in the modern world. We had a lot of witches to design and we had a "witch workshop" using all kinds of references from all different periods. We looked at photographs and said, "In all these historical photographs and costume books filled with people, who is a witch?" We could be looking at a royal wedding from 18-something and think "Which one of them looks like a witch?" We were inspired by the details, a 1930s' hat that's a little bit "too much like that" or somebody who had rather strange dangling sleeves. Michael O'Connor, now an award-winning designer in his own right, was totally key to my being able to do this film, as I was attempting the impossible by trying to do two films at once.

My assistant costume designer on several films, Jacqueline Durran, and I used to talk about whom we'd like to work with and I had seen **Memento** (2000), directed by Christopher Nolan. We used to say, "He's got an interesting vision of things." One day she said, "Christopher Nolan's giving a lecture, you've got to come!" and I said, "I can't go, I'm filming." Jacqueline came back and said, "You've got to work with him. He knows everything about costume; he talks the same language as you.

You've got to work with him." Some years later I got a call to meet him. I went for the interview and got the job [**Batman Begins** (2005)]. At this grand old age it's really thrilling to work in a genre where I get the opportunity to design things using modern technology. I love learning new things, and being on the cutting edge of design because of **Batman** has been such a pleasure.

I am a very fortunate person because I've worked with people who truly care. Ever since I worked in the theater I have developed an active desire to explain to people what costume designers do because I feel that we've been treated as secondary members of the whole process. I found that at the beginning people just treated you like a knickers washer, or they would say, "They're so bossy!" Most costume designers have such a passion for what they are doing that they can't help but make a contribution; therefore, they expect to be respected. The one indispensable quality a costume designer must have is patience, because the things that we have to do are quite crazy most of the time. If we're impatient we won't get anything done. We need bossiness and an "eye" as I call it. There is something about being the costume designer that means we want to impose our vision by kindness or cruelty or strength or gentleness, or whatever means available. The designer must want this very much or wouldn't be bothered to go through all the things that we take, and all the hoops that we have to jump through to get our own way. Well, to try to get our own way. And yes, torture is involved. "

THE DARK KNIGHT

(01–02) "Working with director Chris Nolan on designing The Joker (Heath Ledger) for **The Dark Knight** was a really rewarding, collaborative experience. After lots of discussion about our ideas of who the character might be and why a person would, or could, end up with his appearance, I started researching. I searched for images of earlier Jokers in comics and graphic novels, punk musicians, new romantics, dandies of all types, Francis Bacon's paintings, adding in aged clowns with running greasepaint, and fashion influences from designers Alexander McQueen and Vivienne Westwood. I showed them to Heath and Chris and we had more discussion. Then, very excited, I sat down in a hotel room in West Hollywood, and drew four versions complete with hair, makeup, everything. After that, there was only one change, the color of his waistcoat. The Joker costume was dyed, tailored by hand, and distressed in our costume workshop. His tie was made in Jermyn Street, his socks specially made, and his lovely shoes were made in Italy. His gloves came from Alexander McQueen. Obviously, due to the number of action sequences and stunts, this costume had to be made in many multiples."

03 Hemming's illustrations showing The Joker's gang in **The Dark Knight Rises**

Elizabeth Haffenden

Elizabeth Haffenden was born in Croydon, England in 1906, where she attended the Croydon School of Art, and later London's Royal College of Art. After working as a commercial artist, she became a costume designer for theater and film in the 1930s. Haffenden's first film was **Colonel Blood** (1934), which began her career-long association with historical period epics. In the mid-1930s, she worked (uncredited) alongside the established costume designer René Hubert on several Alexander Korda films before she became part of the British branch of the French studio Gaumont in 1939. The turning point in her career came when she was appointed director of the costume department at Gainsborough Studios, which became known for its flamboyant period melodramas. At

Gainsborough, Haffenden was encouraged to reinterpret stylistically the period by producer R.J. Minney who instructed his creative team, "One must not copy; one must adapt and evolve." Haffenden's designs for the studio include **Love Story** (1944), **The Wicked Lady** (1945), **Caravan** (1946), and **I'll Be Your Sweetheart** (1945), starring British actress Margaret Lockwood. Her designs for **Caravan** predicted Dior's New Look collection, which came out several years later. Her designs for Gainsborough drew attention to the bodies of her actors helping to popularize the studio's critically derided films with an appreciative audience. However, this approach sometimes backfired, as actress Margaret Lockwood explains about **The Wicked Lady**, "I never thought my dress was particularly

01 Elizabeth Haffenden (left) with color consultant and close friend, Joan Bridge shown in pre-production on **Ben-Hur**

02 Fiddler on the Roof

03 A Man for All Seasons

low-cut until I was told the theater owners were not permitted to show the picture unless the scenes where I was wearing a *décolleté* gown were cut out. You can imagine what that did to the continuity of the story." Still, the studio eagerly used Haffenden's seductive costumes as a marketing tool. These escapist post-war films resonated with audiences at a time when Europe's future remained uncertain.

In the late 1950s, Haffenden became resident costume designer at the MGM British Studios where she designed sweeping period epics like **Beau Brummell** (1954) and **Ben-Hur** (1959), for which she won an Academy Award. **Ben-Hur** was a massive undertaking; Haffenden directed a staff, which manufactured thousands of costumes for the epic. In the book *People Who Make Movies*, journalist Theodore Taylor writes, "England's brilliant Elizabeth Haffenden was hired for MGM's **Ben-Hur** and spent more than a year in preliminary work before the first foot of film moved through the camera in Rome. Throughout the filming, Miss Haffenden and her assistants presided over the **Ben-Hur** wardrobe." He added, "A hundred craftsmen, including

seamstresses, leather makers, armorers, and wardrobe personnel were needed to keep **Ben-Hur** properly attired." At MGM, she partnered with Joan Bridge, a Technicolor consultant whom she had met while at Gainsborough. The two colleagues had an extremely close working relationship and friendship, and were awarded an Academy Award for their designs for **A Man for All Seasons** (1966).

Haffenden enjoyed a successful and tremendously influential career into the 1960s and 1970s, including the critically heralded **Fiddler on the Roof** (1971), and **The Homecoming** (1973). Haffenden had begun pre-production design for **Julia** (1977, later designed by Anthea Sylbert) starring Jane Fonda and Vanessa Redgrave when she passed away in 1976.

04 The Prime of Miss Jean Brodie (1969)

05 Ben-Hur

Joanna Johnston

"When I'm starting a new film, my process involves two things—the object and/or the image. It's very random; the starting point or inspiration can be anything. It finds me or I find it, and it stays with me throughout filming."

Daughter of a creative and sophisticated mother and raised in privileged surroundings, Joanna Johnston secured a job as an assistant at Bermans and Nathans Costumiers in London in 1977. It was not long before she began assisting renowned designers on incredible projects: Anthony Powell on **Death on the Nile** (1978), Tom Rand on **The French Lieutenant's Woman** (1981), and Milena Canonero on **Out of Africa** (1985).

After assisting the best, Johnston was asked by Amblin Entertainment producer Kathleen Kennedy to design a "little" film for Robert Zemeckis, which became the ground-breaking live-action/animated hybrid **Who Framed Roger Rabbit** (1988). Through her close creative collaboration with Zemeckis, Johnston became one of the first costume designers to tackle the cutting-edge technologies of animation and motion capture, like designing the drop-dead red gown for the animated Jessica Rabbit. The pair has made eight films together, including **Death Becomes Her** (1992), **The Polar Express** (2004) and the Academy Award-winning **Forrest Gump** (1994), for which Johnston created the unforgettable plaid shirt, khaki suit and sneakers for Tom Hanks' title character.

Johnston is Steven Spielberg's costume designer of choice and cherished collaborator, working closely together on eight productions, including **Saving Private Ryan** (1998), **Munich** (2005), **War Horse** (2011) and **Lincoln** (2012). Spielberg trusts Johnston to produce character-centric and plot-perfect costumes every single time. Her friendship with producer Kennedy facilitated Johnston's collaboration with M. Night Shyamalan. Her great taste, wit and light touch grace **The Sixth Sense** (1999) and **Unbreakable** (2000). Johnston's impeccable style guaranteed Hugh Grant's hip ensembles for **About A Boy** (2002). She is also a favorite of the discerning director Bryan Singer, designing **Valkyrie** (2008) and **Jack the Giant Killer** (2012).

Joanna Johnston

"When I was growing up my father was firstly in the army and then he went onto work in the Royal Household where part of his job was censoring plays and he was therefore very involved in the London theatrical community. He was constantly going to see openings of theatrical plays and musicals, and dealing with the producers, directors and actors because of his job. My mother was a photographer and her family had been involved in various artistic and political circles. As a woman she was a great explorer in all creative fields and was constantly inventing new projects for all around her. She was fearless in pushing boundaries, not only for herself and me; she never put any blocks on her children or what we could do with our lives. Her family was formidable—her mother was Lady Helen Hardinge, a Cecil by birth, and her father, Alexander Hardinge, had also been in the court of his day working for three Monarchs. My grandmother was a woman of great taste and elegance who had a lot of beautiful clothes made by couture houses in Paris. Going through her wardrobe was an early fascination and a strong memory for me.

Growing up in the country, I went to a strict convent boarding school, which was a tradition in our family, but not really the best fit probably. I felt I was being channeled into a life that was over academic and not artistic enough. So I did the opposite of everything I was told to do and left school at the first opportunity, at 17, wanting to experience everything on the outside. All fairly annoying for my parents, I imagine. Good at sewing and interested in fashion, I didn't want anything more to do with education. I considered art school, but thought it would be too long, laborious and restricting—a complete misjudgment on my part. At the time, I felt the workplace was the way to go. After a course in pattern cutting and design at a private college, I was told that I was "good with my hands."

While I was still at school, Stanley Kubrick was filming **Barry Lyndon** (1975) in various fine country houses, one of which belonged to my aunt in Dorset. After a call from my cousins I was fairly desperate to visit the set, so in time I went over to watch the shooting. I recall Stanley Kubrick was up in the drawing room with my aunt having tea, when I'm sure he was meant to be filming, but he clearly did things at his own speed. It was utterly thrilling to see everybody dressed up in Milena Canonero's gorgeous costumes. She was the first designer I ever met and she just knocked me out. While there I saw her whisk together a hat for a servant boy out of a piece of cardboard, covered it with fabric, then plonked it on his head within ten minutes and then it was immediately being filmed. I was amazed. Milena was so beautiful and looked like she accomplished everything with such ease. Witnessing Milena's hat trick was probably the first real "striker" for me to become a designer, although I didn't realize it at the time. Funnily enough, that day the free food from catering was as important to me as the film production.

After a year of college I wanted to work, but in fashion. I had one job interview that was so awful

01 Meryl Streep as Madeline Ashton in **Death Becomes Her**

> "My designs are character driven. My goal is to make sure that the costumes say exactly who each person is by how they are worn."

I ended up going home crying my eyes out. My brilliant, remarkable mother said, "What about the theatrical world?" I never would have thought of that option myself. My mother pulled rank (with, I think, Frank Muir) and I got a job working with Bermans and Nathans Costumiers that paid £11 a week. At 19 years old it was like an apprenticeship. While working at Bermans, I met various designers including the legendary Irene Sharaff. With Ms. Sharaff, you felt that you were in the presence of greatness. I was quite slim at the time she asked me to model some of her costumes, which made me feel a mixture of excitement and fear. I will never forget her working with the dressmakers in the fitting room; an extraordinary experience.

Two things happened at this time that made me realize I was most interested in film as a medium. Firstly, I had been asked by designer Tom Rand to work with him on a commercial with Ridley Scott, so I took time off and spent a week working with Tom. I really loved being in the thick of a filming environment. The second thing was a conversation my mother had one evening with a friend of hers, the producer John Brabourne. As a result of that conversation I was offered a position to work on his next film, which was **Death on the Nile** (1978), assisting Anthony Powell.

Being very naïve, I never really planned anything; events just happened and fell into place. I never had a structure, but I was very keen to learn. So my first film was **Death on the Nile** with a cast of huge stars. I couldn't quite believe it; it was like being in a dream. Anthony along with Tom Rand both became my mentors, and I couldn't have asked for two more brilliant teachers to learn my craft from. Most of what I apply today I learnt from them.

My launch as a designer was another unexpected situation. I'd assisted Anthony Powell on Steven Spielberg's **Indiana Jones and the Temple of Doom** (1984), which was the first time I had worked with both Spielberg and Kathleen Kennedy. Not long afterwards, Kathleen came →

Finding inspiration in real clothes

(02) "I'm a massive fan of flea market finds; I use them for color, shape, trim, or as a complete outfit. It can be anything. When I designed **Munich** (2005), which is set in the early 1970s, there was still a lot of available stock at a good price and the markets proved to be the best fertile place for early 1970s stay-press clothes. I used a lot of original stock on many of the principal actors. Portobello is my regular stomping ground and I know most of the dealers. Whenever I start on a project they'll ask, 'Okay what are we looking for now?' I'll say, 'I'm looking for whatever it is,' including the date and type. And then the next week there are bundles of items to the requisite that I asked for, often very ravishing pieces. I just love that and going back to the heart of the real clothes. Whether you keep them in their pure form or spring from them, that's the fun isn't it? It's like a mixing box."

02

to London and asked if I was interested in working on a "small film that Steven was producing and a protégé of his was directing." She thought it too small for Anthony to design so the offer went to me. The film was **Who Framed Roger Rabbit** (1988), directed by Bob [Robert] Zemeckis. It may have started out small, but it ended up something quite different. **Who Framed Roger Rabbit** bridged traditional hand-drawn animation to the new world of computer technology being done at Industrial Light & Magic (ILM). It was just at the beginning of this transition and I remember the sound of the animators' paper flicking back and forth as they

worked. Bob Zemeckis is always pushing his films technically and every time we've worked together we've ventured into new territory.

Every day we had massive challenges like how a cartoon penguin waiter was going to carry a real tray of real drinks and give it to a real actor in the scene. Working on **Who Framed Roger Rabbit** was like being on the best game show ever on an hour-by-hour basis. Designing only the live action I didn't have anything to do with the cartoons apart from designing Jessica Rabbit. Based on Rita Hayworth in **Gilda** (1946), I decided on a super hot pink sequined gown. It was too expensive to animate her sequins all the

FORREST GUMP

(01) "Forrest (Tom Hanks) is on his way back to see Jenny (Robin Wright), who he loves more than life itself. His suit is a very lightweight seersucker fabric. He is wearing the Nikes that Jenny had given him some years previously, which were a model that came out in 1978 when athletic wear was just coming into its own. Forrest has run across North America three times already so they were trashed and I thought it was a very 'Forrest' thing that he would put in new laces 'in honor' of Jenny, which makes them look quirky to say the least. The socks were hand knitted and are a style that goes back to his childhood. I came up with a style that Forrest held onto when everyone else changed with the trends, chinos, checked shirts with hard pressed short sleeves and clean socks. The shirt was a blue check that I designed to look as if it was made cheaply in Taiwan. My shirt maker kept matching the checks, as any good tailor would. Finally, we had to lay out the mismatched pattern together." **(02, 04)** "I was having a bit of a crisis about the big protest scene in Washington coming up in the schedule with Jenny's (Robin Wright) clothes, which were designed around an Afghani velvet coat that had come out of my grandmother's closet. Director Bob Zemeckis decided that he wanted Jenny to go into the water at the Lincoln Memorial. We needed so many doubles that I didn't know how I was going to get all the embroidery repeated, which is now very funny, as the bus stop scene is so iconic I wish that I had been able to just relish it at the time." **(02–03)** Illustrations by Robin Richesson. **(05)** Sally Field as Mrs. Gump.

time in the film, so Jessica only had sequins sparkling when she was performing. To determine what color the sequins would reflect onto the people's faces when she was on stage, I had to do a mock-up of color and shine on cloth as a reference. Everything about the design of that dress defied gravity; it could never be accomplished for a human. And Jessica Rabbit was the best-behaved actress.

When I'm starting a new film, my process involves two things—the object and/or the image. It's very random; the starting point or inspiration can be anything. It finds me or I find it, and the object or the image stays with me throughout the filming. When I was designing **Unbreakable** (2000), a contemporary film, I found a portrait from the 1860s of Franz Xaver Winterhalter of this guy with the weirdest sideways hair that started my creative process for Samuel L. Jackson's character. When I read the script for **War Horse** (2011), I recalled a photograph of my grandmother's older brother, George Cecil, mounted on his horse in his Grenadier uniform just before World War I. The horse is coming forward, ears pricked; George is in profile, turning to see what's behind him. He looks resplendent in his uniform, optimistic and healthy, with all his kit perfectly turned out. By Christmas, he'd been killed just before his 19th birthday. I had his photograph with me through **War Horse,** →

because it was so evocative of the time as well as the personal story.

Early in the process when it's just me, or with one or two people on the costume crew, it's the calm before the storm. I'm shuffling about creating my own perspective on the story to be told. Then, when I think I'm going down one creative track, I might find something else really interesting that pulls the project in a way that I hadn't previously considered. My designs are character-driven. My goal is to make sure that the costumes say exactly who each person is by how they are worn. And that the audience can recognize the character just through sight. Mostly, my creative contribution includes a lot of nuance that sometimes goes unnoticed by the public.

The costume designer's job starts with discussions with the director. From there I usually create mood boards as a starting point based on that meeting; this will give the director something to react to, which then gives me the confidence to go forward into the main design process. Working with a sketch artist, the designs are then presented to the director and actors. Once these are approved the process of fabric buying, dyeing, printing and pattern cutting starts. I never show the director anything during the process, as I prefer the total "illusion" of a completed costume. Costumes are part of the big puzzle of the image so ideally they are best seen set within the whole space they will finally inhabit. If the costume is isolated and out of context, it can be detrimental. An actor walking on set for the first time in their full glory of costume, hair and makeup can be incredibly interesting and exciting, and seeing the reactions of crew and other cast, as well as the emotions of the actor is great to witness. Watching that moment always seems to deny the passage of time, it must have been the same from the beginning of Hollywood.

Previous to that moment, the fitting-room process for me is fairly private and personal, and I'm probably a bit overprotective within this area—building trust with the actor, and then making the magic of the character I think is an intimate time.

Then with the collaboration of the incredible talent that I have had the privilege to work with, where you can ask for something that would take the normal world a few months to produce, but here is created in near-finished form within a day or two for the fitting, it never ceases to amaze me. Also the merging of ideas with the actor can be fantastic. When I was designing **Forrest Gump** (1994), I came up with the idea that Forrest's personality was a result of living with his proud mother in the Deep South. This would manifest itself through his buttoned-up shirts and his disciplined precision and neatness. Tom Hanks came to the fitting room as a blank piece of paper; it was early days and he hadn't really formed a lot of the nuances of the man in his head at this point, so the character seemed to somewhat evolve in the fitting room in front of us with the application of the clothes on the artist. The voice started coming and through the process of the 80-something changes that he had to wear, gave the springboard for Forrest—it was a sweet merger of creative thought. During one fitting Tom started dancing to show a Forrest-type dance. It was utterly brilliant, it completely melted the room. It's the one he does when he dances with Jenny in the film.

The other collaboration I totally enjoy is with the art department. It's the department I get most involved with and I seem to love all the production designers and art directors that I have worked with. The most long-lasting collaboration has been with Rick Carter and we have worked together for 11 films now. Our communication can be super quick as we just "know."

It seems that often the most challenging projects are the war films, of which I've now designed four: **Saving Private Ryan** (1998), **Valkyrie** (2008), **War Horse** (2011) and **Lincoln** (2012). It's about honoring the look of them, for the people who know or remember. But as ever you are only as good as the people who work alongside you, and in all the military work I've done, the brilliant David Crossman gives me a two-year degree course in a matter of weeks →

01

01 Valkyrie

02 War Horse

03 Tom Sizemore and Tom Hanks in **Saving Private Ryan**

WHO FRAMED ROGER RABBIT

(04) "**Who Framed Roger Rabbit** was my first film; but it was the most remarkable experience, in a precious time being at the cusp of the old technology moving into digital. Eddie Valiant (Bob Hoskins) was very ordinary, a guy who would more often sleep in his clothes, but was trying to keep up appearances. His suit was made of lightweight cloth appropriate for California, half-lined and constructed in a box-like shape. Bob Zemeckis, who directed the film, said that he thought guys who wore brown suits looked like losers. Jessica Rabbit went through several design processes in body, hair and clothes. Bob Zemeckis asked me to design some clothes and her hair to pull her more into our world of the 1940s. Jessica's look is based on Rita Hayworth in **Gilda** (1946), which, when it is 'poured' on the body of Jessica, defeats all logical construction. I thought that it should be a very hot color and did Schiaparelli pink, which in the daytime scenes was drawn as just a silk satin and when she performs on stage is covered in sequins. We couldn't afford to have sequins all the way through the film, which I would have liked, because the process at the time was too expensive."

01–02 Robin Richesson's illustrations for "Elijah" and how this was interpreted in **Unbreakable** with the help of Samuel L. Jackson

02 UNBREAKABLE — SAMUEL L. JACKSON — ELIJAH —

INT LIMITED EDITION —   EXT. STADIUM —   INT PHYSICAL THERAPY CENTER —

and makes the ideas materialize in a very remarkable way. I am the daughter of a military man so it must be in my blood, and through the process of doing these projects I have come to really enjoy and get satisfaction in the military work, which has surprised me as I would never have thought I would have satisfaction in this field at the beginning of my career. On **Saving Private Ryan** my father—who fought at the end of World War II aged 19—came to the set a few times and managed to tell Steven Spielberg that the scenes were totally realistic; it was really sweet the bridging of the worlds.

When working for the same directors you develop trust and a shorthand, and I love that. That's my relationship with Bob Zemeckis, because we've collaborated on so many films. Right now, I'm designing **Jack the Giant Killer** (2012), a fantasy film for director Bryan Singer, who I worked with previously on **Valkyrie**. Bryan gives me total creative freedom and that's so lucky. For **Jack the Giant Killer** I have rolled over most of my costume crew from the production of **War Horse**. I don't ever remember having done this before and this has been a huge asset. The crew and I have such a strong connection and my team is absolutely the top of the pile. Creatively, working like this is remarkable.

Designing costumes for film has changed as the technology has changed and I have been very lucky to be on the crest of the wave of the new technologies. I'm not fearful that technology is going to take over because I believe our work will still carry on. We costume designers just have to navigate our way and figure out how it can work for us. I like working with the visual effects people and I hope that we'll interface more as time goes on. Designers understand how the cloth is going to move and fall. Instead of CGI having to figure it out, we can do the shorthand because we have the expertise. Producers and directors need to understand that it's an advantage to the film to include the costume designer in these conversations.

I like this idea of cooperative filmmaking; for me that would be a complete perfect thing. I would be at the table incorporating the costume design process from the very beginning of the story concept. This would be so exciting, because the designer would be an integrated part of a production, rather than (as today) a hired hand. There would be less of the existing hierarchy on a production, and the costume designer would be treated with respect and as a creative equal. I heard director Baz Luhrmann on the radio some years ago, talking about the time he directed **Romeo + Juliet** (1996). He said that after he completes the first draft of his script he takes his key "creatives" (the editor, production designer, costume designer, DP) for a think-tank, brainstorming week somewhere lovely like a tropical island. He said, "What is so nice is that everybody puts their ideas on the table and everybody's on the same footing." That idea—that even playing field with everybody involved and respectful—I love that. I don't know why it can't happen; it's so simple.

THE POLAR EXPRESS

(03–04) According to Johnston, this "was the first full-length motion-capture film. Director Bob Zemekis decided that it would be greatly beneficial for me to design and make actual costumes because they would serve as the blueprint for the computer-generated clothes. Presented on a human form for 3D scanning, there were details that I had to restrain myself from adding due to the cost of computerization. Design restrictions can also be liberating. For instance, I designed the 'Hero Boy' clothing on a child, but the character was played by Tom Hanks, who also played the Conductor, Santa Claus and the Hobo, and I made all of those costumes for him. Costume designers and the CGI world need each other and it has been brilliant to be involved from the outset. It's a different platform, but ultimately the role is the same for the costume designer." **(04)** Illustration by Robin Richesson.

Michael Kaplan

"For me, being a costume designer is instinctual. When I start a project, although I've read the script and have a feeling about the atmosphere I want, I can't verbalize it."

Michael Kaplan exhibited artistic promise from an early age and received a scholarship to study drawing and sculpture at the Philadelphia College of Art. After graduation, Kaplan moved to Los Angeles and worked as an illustrator for legendary television costume designers Bob Mackie and Ret Turner. He also assisted designer Bob De Mora on **American Hot Wax** (1978) and designed a stage show for Bette Midler.

Ridley Scott's seminal **Blade Runner** (1982) was Kaplan's first film, which he co-designed with Charles Knode. The BAFTA Award-winning costumes for Scott's dystopian future drew heavily from the 1940s. Kaplan's next film, **Flashdance** (1983), featured Jennifer Beals in a bare-shouldered gray sweatshirt and leg warmers, a look that instantly became iconic. In the next decade, Kaplan would design the murder-mystery comedy **Clue** (1985); the Bette Midler/Lily Tomlin farce, **Big Business** (1988); and the perennial holiday favorite, **National Lampoon's Christmas Vacation** (1989).

In the mid-1990s, Kaplan designed **Se7en** (1995), the first of four films on which he has collaborated with director David Fincher. Fincher's stylish and gleefully anarchic **Fight Club** (1999), starring Edward Norton as an emasculated malcontent and Brad Pitt as his sex-fueled alter ego, allowed Kaplan the full range of character creation.

Since 2000, Kaplan has excelled in every genre. With his credits including Michael Bay's World War II drama **Pearl Harbor** (2001); followed by his third film with Brad Pitt, the action comedy **Mr. & Mrs. Smith** (2005); J. J. Abrams' reboot of the sci-fi classic **Star Trek** (2009); and the crystallized musical **Burlesque** (2010), starring Christina Aguilera and Cher, Kaplan continues to stretch his creative horizons.

Michael Kaplan

"My interest in costume started early. I recall an event when I was four years old. One Christmas holiday I went to Miami Beach with my family. At the hotel they had an informal modeling show around the pool. There's a Super 8 home movie of me running after a model, grabbing her dress and not letting go. The beautiful fabrics fascinated me. In elementary school, I would tell my mother what to wear to parent-teacher nights, like her spectator shoes; then I would just beam when the teachers told me how beautiful she looked. My mother is still a great beauty at 87.

Growing up in Germantown, an area of Philadelphia, I had a strong need to express myself artistically and was reprimanded for drawing on the walls. In his youth, my father was very talented as an artist and had been given a full scholarship to Cooper Union, but had to turn it down because of the Depression. Instead he worked to help support his family. He encouraged me to follow my artistic dreams and experience what he had not been able to. I too was awarded a full scholarship to Philadelphia College of Art (which is now the University of the Arts), where I studied drawing and sculpture, and took some classes in illustration. I was an adept draftsman.

After college I didn't feel I had the right temperament to get up every morning and make fine art, so I went from company to company doing commercial graphic design, illustration and designing book jackets. But it wasn't satisfying and I didn't want to stay in Philadelphia. It dawned on me that I kept thinking about costume design—even back when I was a kid, I remember seeing **The Girl in the Red Velvet Swing** (1955, costumes designed by Charles LeMaire), a period film about architect Stanford White in which Joan Collins played his paramour (Evelyn Nesbit, The Gibson Girl). I remember being struck by the extravagant period costumes. Once I decided that costume design was my true calling, I put together a portfolio

BLADE RUNNER

(01–02) Kaplan's sketch for a quilted coat with faux fur for the character "Rachel" and how it appeared on screen as worn by Sean Young. **(03–04)** "This suit for Rachel, played by Sean Young, was inspired by the tailoring of [Gilbert] Adrian in the 1940s. Although **Blade Runner** takes place in the future, we wanted a 1940s' film noir feeling to it."

01

of costume sketches from various periods drawn in different styles, things that I copied from books as well as things that I invented, and without hesitation I moved to Los Angeles.

Once I settled in, I went to interviews, meeting different designers in search of work as a sketch artist. One of the people I met was Edith Head, who said, "Lovely, lovely drawings. I don't need a sketch artist right now, but I'll certainly keep you in mind. It'll be just a matter of time before you start working." She advised me, "Try to do everything that's offered to you. You don't know what it's going to turn into." I did sketches for some working costume designers and would-be designers.

Calvin Klein was a friend of mine from the East Coast who knew my drawings; he'd taught me so much about simplicity and design. Calvin called Bob Mackie on my behalf and I set up an interview to show him my drawings at Elizabeth Courtney Costumes—Mackie's home base. "We don't need anybody, but we'll certainly keep you in mind," they said, recalling Ms. Head. A few

weeks later they phoned to tell me that Ret Turner (Bob's associate costume designer) had an assistant leaving to go out on her own. They asked me to fill her position. That's when I first met the brilliant Julie Weiss; she was clearing out her desk when I started. My duties were assisting and sketching for Ret on **The Sonny & Cher Show**, as well as gophering for Ray Aghayan, Bob, and anyone else who needed assistance. They would send me out to International Silks and Woolens to get three yards of black taffeta or hammered satin. I would walk around the store and look at tags until I found what I was searching for, embarrassed to admit that I had no idea what these things were. Even for very simple things, I'd be gone for an hour and a half. I worked for all of them doing things like coloring shoes to match dresses, or shopping for buttons. That was my first real job in the business and it got me into Local 705. An amazing education!

Working at Elizabeth Courtney was a Who's Who of the musical stars of Las Vegas and live →

television; someone famous would always be walking in the door—Diana Ross, Mitzi Gaynor, Carol Burnett, Steve and Eydie, and Cher. The Jackson Five were guest stars on **The Sonny & Cher Show**, and I sketched little Michael's costumes. Tina Turner had bodyguards around her dressing room after Ike made death threats. What a crazy atmosphere for a kid from Philadelphia to be in within a year of coming to Los Angeles.

Amazing as it was working for Mackie and Ret Turner, I didn't want to get trapped in TV. I wanted to work in movies. Bob De Mora, an old pal of Bette Midler's who'd designed a lot of stage work for her early in her career, took me under his wing so I could learn the ropes. Bob hired me to assist him on **American Hot Wax** (1978), a movie about the pop music scandals going on in radio in the 1950s that featured musicians Chuck Berry and Jerry Lee Lewis as themselves. Bob's designs had grittiness, a handmade quality. He liked a certain tawdriness that I think he learned when he assisted Ann Roth. It separates a costume from looking like a costume to becoming something that takes you into a different reality. When I look at my designs for **Fight Club** (1999) and **Burlesque** (2010), Bob's influence on me is apparent.

For me, being a costume designer is instinctual. When I start a project, although I've read the script and have an idea about the atmosphere I want, I can't verbalize it. Color is in my head, but if you asked me what colors I'd like to use I wouldn't know. So I generally go to a favorite vintage store and select clothes I gravitate to by instinct that might be right for extras, or special pieces that might inspire me, to clarify what's in my mind and get a sense of color and a look that I'll usually stick with throughout the project. I don't even look at the clothes rack until I've finished completely going through the shop, and a lot of the things I pull never go on an actor, but then somehow I understand, "Oh, that's what I'm doing." Once I have a better idea and have defined the research period, I begin sketching. On **Pearl Harbor** (2001), I didn't

want the clothes to be from 1941, even though the attack happened that year; I wanted the clothes to be from 1938–39. The fashions wouldn't be so up to the minute on the characters I would be describing in the film. I make all these determinations and then start putting things together.

Of course it's important to listen carefully to the director. David Fincher doesn't like clothes to stand out and he doesn't like a lot of color. When I was designing **Fight Club** I knew he would generally be horrified by red. So I remember saying to him, "I keep thinking about red for Tyler Durden; how far can I go?" David told me to follow my instincts: "You can't go too far with Tyler Durden." Brad Pitt was playing the role and wasn't clear on what Tyler Durden should look like. It was a strange movie because we were dealing with a level of unreality—people who weren't real, but still had to look and seem real. Brad is a great collaborator; we'd worked together on **Se7en** (1995) so I knew that he's really open to fresh ideas. We had so much fun with things that I found in thrift shops, although most of what we needed would have to be →

02–03 Pearl costume for Christina Aguilera. "The costume needed to 'fly' off her in a striptease number. Quite a design feat!" Illustration by Brian Valenzuela

04–05 Kaplan says he designed this "surrealistic" hands costume for Christina also. "It was one of her favorites!" Illustration by Brian Valenzuela

BURLESQUE

(02–05) "**Burlesque** was the hardest film I've ever designed. There were about 20 musical numbers on a ten-week shoot. It boiled down to shooting two musical numbers a week as well as the rest of the non-musical movie. All of the costumes and shoes were made to order; hundreds of fittings."

"Working with Bob Mackie was a Who's Who of the musical stars of Las Vegas and live television; someone famous would always be walking in the door."

manufactured in multiples, because they were constantly being damaged or destroyed in the fight scenes. They needed to look as though they were secondhand, so I would have them produced in the workroom, then age them, breaking buttons, cracking leather, putting things in the oven, dyeing and washing them, so they looked 30 years old even though they were actually made the week before. I even remember stapling on a price tag and ripping it off, leaving a slight remnant.

Working with actors more than once is great because you know the way they like to work. It takes away the formality at the beginning. Any time you work with somebody brand new, you want to get off to a good start, you want to have the best experience possible, and everybody has a different way of working. You hear horror stories about this one or that one being difficult. For the most part I ignore these stories because I've found that usually those people are perfectionists who care about what they're doing—to me that's not difficult; that's a plus.

When Charles Knode and I were designing **Blade Runner** (1982) for Ridley Scott, Harrison Ford had been cast late and we had already done all of these sketches of his character wearing a futuristic trench coat and the strange suit. In one sketch the character was wearing a kind of futuristic Humphrey Bogart fedora. "I've just finished a movie," said Harrison Ford. "It's not out yet, but I wore a hat through the whole thing. I don't want to wear a hat." The sketches were for Harrison to look at and say "yay" or "nay," so the hat idea was discarded. The film he was referring to was, of course, **Raiders of the Lost Ark** (1981, costumes designed by Deborah Nadoolman). →

01–03 Kaplan consulting with Jennifer Beals on the set of **Flashdance**. "The cut of the sweatshirt seemed like an appropriate garment for a welder/dancer who read *Italian Vogue*." Illustration by Pauline Annon

JENNIFER BEALS
"FLASH DANCE"

How costumes create a character

(04–07) "**Fight Club** was a great script, the performers were extraordinary, and I think I was really suited for the job. Of all the films I've designed, that's my favorite because I enjoyed the cast and crew, and the process so much. And the edginess! When we were just starting, Helena Bonham Carter called me from London and said, 'I don't know what this movie is about. I have no idea who Marla Singer is. I'll be there in a week or so and hopefully you can help me with the character. In the meantime, do you have anything at all I can be thinking about? What's your take on Marla Singer?' Without pausing I said, 'Judy Garland for the Millennium.' She roared and that's what I did. It's who Helena was. In fact, David Fincher called her Judy throughout the shoot."

04–05 Helena Bonham Carter as Marla Singer. Illustration by Pauline Annon

06–07 Brad Pitt as Tyler Durden in **Fight Club**. "I've never used this much color in a male actor in a film. Director David Fincher told me, 'you can't go too far.' Here you can see how I contrasted the palettes of Brad Pitt's and Edward Norton's clothes. I also needed to manufacture the thrift-shop look, since multiples were needed for the fight scenes." Illustration by Pauline Annon

01

STARFLEET CADETS

02

SPOCK

03

ENTERPRISE

04

ROMULAN

05

06

STAR TREK

(01–08) "These cadet uniforms were a hit with director J. J. Abrams. I wanted to create a look that was both youthful and a homage to the 1960s when **Star Trek** began (01, 06, 08)." (02) "Mr. Spock's spherical hood was very complex in its construction because I wanted it to collapse into a collar when taken down. It ended up becoming one of my favorite costumes in the film." (03, 07) The revamped Enterprise uniforms. "I had fabric printed with lots of tiny Star Trek logos to add a textured effect." (04) Eric Bana as the Romulan Nero. (05) A draped suit for Leonard Nimoy as Spock Prime. Illustrations by Brian Valenzuela.

"What's most important is creating the character with costume. That's where the need for simplicity comes in; if you have too much going on, it's confusing."

People say you should always check with the production designer early on to see what he's doing, because you don't want to have an actress in a red dress sitting on a red sofa. But that's kind of a joke; it's usually not an issue. Although I do practice normal etiquette with the production designer and receive swatches or room colors. There's generally a broader harmony that's not about the color of the upholstery in the room.

On **Star Trek** (2009) I worked with production designer Scott Chambliss. We didn't check in that often, but when we did talk we were almost always on the same track. We both had frequent meetings with J. J. Abrams, our gifted director, and we knew we wanted to do a **Star Trek** that would be in the correct vernacular, but wouldn't copy anything from the original per se. We would reboot it for this new generation.

From time to time there might be an entire scene that is being shot in close-up, and you can't see much of the costume. I try to have conversations with the cinematographer beforehand to say, "This is a very special costume that needs to be seen for these reasons. If we can, we should show it from the feet up." Sometimes they haven't thought about it; you need to bring it to their attention, but once you mention it, the cinematographer is usually as accommodating as possible. What's most important is creating the character with costume. That's where the need for simplicity comes in; if you have too much going on, it's confusing. You go through all the choices and hone it down to what defines the character you're creating. A costume designer must be relentless in that the costume has to be correct. You don't stop or settle until it is right. Julie Weiss has that drive more than anybody I've met. It's important. There are times when I've changed things even after the camera started rolling, just to make it perfect, because once it's shot, it's shot. Until then, you strive for the right note.

The film business has changed and there are only huge commercial movies and very small movies that have incredibly tiny budgets—nothing in between. So many of the films that I've designed in the past couldn't be made today, including **Fight Club**. It wasn't that easy for Fincher to make it even when he did; it was a labor of love made through sheer tenacity.

Costume designers don't start out to set a fashion trend, but sometimes it happens. At the time the movie came out, **Flashdance** (1983) set a huge trend, and it keeps coming back; stylists and fashion designers reference it and say 1980s' fashion is coming back in the mode of **Flashdance**. Pretty recently Jennifer Lopez did a music video that David LaChapelle directed. They reproduced a lot of the costumes and dance numbers from **Flashdance**—although billed as an homage, it was a total "lift." The designer, Marc Jacobs, who's a friend of mine, called me a number of years ago and said he was designing a collection that once again, paid homage to **Flashdance**. Donatella Versace designed an entire **Fight Club** menswear collection just after the movie came out with all the models looking like Tyler Durden, with shaved heads and wearing fur coats and graphic T-shirts. Alexander McQueen did a **Blade Runner** collection that was on the cover of *Italian Vogue*. When I passed the newsstand I thought it was a still from the movie. For whatever reason, these three movies are so iconic; they keep coming back into the consciousness of the style mavens.

A director once said to me, "We want you to design this movie and set a trend the same way you did on **Flashdance**." I pointed out that he had responsibility in this too. "Really? How so?" he asked, and I answered, "the movie has to be a huge hit." Show me a trend set by a movie that wasn't a huge hit—**Bonnie and Clyde**, **Annie Hall** and **It Happened One Night**…

Good designers work the same way on hits and flops. **"**

MR. & MRS. SMITH

(01–03) "My fun daily routine of holding Angie 'in' as her rubber corset was laced up (02)." Angelina Jolie as Jane Smith (01). "The challenge of this costume was that the director wanted the coat to flair out like a parachute as Jane descended from her jump off the rooftop terrace. There is steel framework in the skirt of the coat."

Judianna Makovsky

"Costume designers design a whole character. The process starts with the script. I try to find character and then the world they live in. After that, I do the research, and then I design the clothes. For me, that process pretty much stays that way every time."

Born in New Jersey, Judianna Makovsky earned her BFA from the Art Institute of Chicago, followed by an MFA from Yale School of Drama. Her film career began in the mid-1980s, when she assisted the great Milena Canonero on Francis Ford Coppola's **The Cotton Club** (1984) and the visually stunning, **Dick Tracy** (1990). Makovsky's first solo costume design credit was Coppola's **Gardens of Stone** (1987), followed by Penny Marshall's classic comedy **Big** (1988), for which she designed the unforgettable white tie and tails for Tom Hanks.

Makovsky's work is a veritable smorgasbord of classic genre. She's designed it all, and brilliantly. She designed the accurate period costumes for Robert Redford's 1930s golf film, **The Legend of Bagger Vance** (2000), Alfonso Cuarón's attentive film adaptation of **A Little Princess** (1995), Sam Raimi's stylized western **The Quick and the Dead** (1995) and Taylor Hackford's supernatural thriller **The Devil's Advocate** (1997). The flawless, black-and-white-to-color 1950s' costumes she designed for Gary Ross's **Pleasantville** (1998) earned her an Academy Award nomination. Ross's **Seabiscuit** (2003), from Laura Hillenbrand's inspiring book about the depression-era racehorse, brought her a second nomination.

Makovsky designed both Jon Turteltaub's action-adventure hits **National Treasure** (2004) and its sequel, **National Treasure: Book of Secrets** (2007). She designed M. Night Shyamalan's **The Last Airbender** (2010), and co-designed (with Lisa Tomczeszyn) the super-hero extravaganza **X-Men: The Last Stand** (2006). She made movie history as the designer of **Harry Potter and the Sorcerer's Stone** (2001), forever establishing the look of the juggernaut franchise. Her now iconic Hogwarts uniforms earned her another Academy Award nomination and legions of fans forever.

Judianna Makovsky

"My mother taught music after she gave up her career as a concert pianist to marry my pediatrician father. When I was five my father died and although we lived in Jersey City, New Jersey, my mother put my brother in the children's chorus, and me in the ballet and later the children's chorus, at the Metropolitan Opera. This commitment got me out of elementary school early often at least four days a week and I made money, which was a fabulous thing. Even though I liked performing I was more interested in what went on backstage and by 17, I knew I wasn't going to be a dancer. I loved the theater and opera and ballet, and I wanted to be a designer.

Growing up at the Met, I recognized that opera was one kind of very theatrical design. In elementary school and high school, I saw films like director Franco Zeffirelli's **Romeo and Juliet** (1968, costumes designed by Danilo Donati) and costume designer Piero Tosi's **The Leopard** (1963), and designer Anthony Powell's **Travels with My Aunt** (1972) that inspired me, because each designer took costumes into the realm of creating characters through clothing. At school I took a lot of art classes because I believed that in order to be a designer you had to be an artist first, and that I needed the whole package: an art school background and theater school background.

A LITTLE PRINCESS

(01–02) "A wonderful challenge to create a world that is defined by one specific color—green. The difficulty was to make it believable and not a cartoon." Makovsky saw this as a challenge and her enthusiasm in this approach got her the job.

> "At school I took a lot of art classes because I believed that in order to be a designer you had to be an artist first, and that I needed the whole package."

I went to the School of the Art Institute of Chicago (SAIC), which at that time owned the Goodman School of Drama, and I majored in painting, drawing and textile arts at the Institute and minored in costume design at the Goodman. During my last year, I was sent to NYC to the first TDF Portfolio review as Goodman's representative. There I met set designer and Yale professor Ming Cho Lee, who reviewed our portfolios. "You're not supposed to be here, this is only for graduate students," he told me, "but you're incredibly talented." And he invited me to come to Yale even though I'd already accepted an offer by the Bristol Old Vic in England. When I got to Bristol they wanted me to be a set designer and I really wanted to be a costume designer, so I left, took a year off and accepted Ming's invitation to Yale.

At Yale, I met Jane Greenwood, the head of the costume design program and a most amazing human being. In addition to teaching, Jane manages to design shows both on and off Broadway, for opera and ballet all over the world, and have a fabulous family life. From Yale, I was very lucky to go right to work for Jane and then through her I got a call from the great costume designer Milena Canonero, who asked me to assist her on an opera at the Met. She said she'd got my number from Anthony Powell, whom I'd never met! When I had to turn down Milena, who designed →

03 The Quick and the Dead
"Since this western is a fable, I wanted to do a romanticized vision of a western and not a particularly period-specific one. I also wanted it to be the dirtiest, dustiest and grimiest of westerns. Fun!"

GREAT EXPECTATIONS
(**04**) "Another opportunity to work with Alfonso Cuarón's favorite color green to create mood and to have a stylized, but believable world for the characters to exist in. I love to control palette, and make each frame a painting."

God is in the detail

(01–05) "The details and the process are not always seen on the big screen. In **Harry Potter and the Sorcerer's Stone**, the ghost costumes including Nearly Headless Nick are amongst my favorites **(01–03)**. Every piece of trim on Nick's Elizabethan costume was stenciled on sheer ribbon, every button embroidered. I wanted something that was not the usual floating white ghosts. It had to be substantial and ethereal at the same time, also period accurate. Finding the right base fabric was the clue. Noel Howard at MBA costumes who made most of the costumes was my collaborator on these and he found a gray open mesh with threads of copper that could be manipulated into folds and creases."

04–05 Makovsky's illustrations showing costumes for Richard Harris as Professor Albus Dumbledore and Dame Maggie Smith as Professor Minerva McGonagall

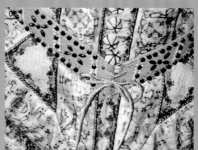

Barry Lyndon (1975) and **Chariots of Fire** (1981), because I was designing a show at Indiana Repertory Theater, I was convinced that I'd ruined my entire career because by then I knew that I wanted to design for film instead of theater.

Luckily, Milena called me again when she came to New York to design **The Cotton Club** (1984) for Francis Ford Coppola. Richard Shissler (another assistant designer) and I were thrown into this enormous movie, but I easily took to the scale and the size of it. Milena and I got on famously and we had so much fun playing with these incredible vintage garments that came from Europe, the likes of which I'd never seen. We continued to work together on a few projects and when the designer of Francis Coppola's **Gardens of Stone** (1987) left in the middle of the film, Milena recommended to Francis that I take over as costume designer.

Then I was hired to assist Santo Loquasto on **Big** (1988). We'd worked together when Santo was the production designer on **Radio Days** (1987)—he'd designed all the Woody Allen movies—and I'd assisted the costume designer Jeffrey Kurland. A few weeks after I started he said to me, "I've seen what you did with Milena and Jeffrey. I went to the producers and Penny Marshall and told them that I'll just design the sets and you'll design the costumes. And so have your first movie. Congratulations." I was terrified,

but so happy to have my first full movie.

As an assistant, I worked with directors like Woody Allen and Francis Ford Coppola and Warren Beatty, so I had very high standards. But every director is different and they all work differently, although in a funny way the really good directors all have the same process. Still, you have a new learning curve on every project. For me, everything starts with the script. Immediately I get images in my head of where I want to go with the design. Then I talk with the director, to see if that's his image and discuss his ideas. Sometimes directors are visual and they have a vision for the film; and sometimes they're not. At that point, I look through the 52 boxes of picture files that I've been collecting since high school, trying to find images that inspire me for the project. And now, with the Internet, you can research anything. Then I talk with the production designer and see what kind of world these people live in, and the clothes are almost the last step in the design process. A lot of directors aren't interested in the clothes, the individual garments; they're more interested in character and the visuals of the whole world of the script. Things change when the actor gets involved and naturally, they have their own opinions.

Costume designers design a whole character. The process starts with the script. I try to find character and then the world they live in. After

BIG

(06) "This was my first full design job for film and I was so lucky to start out on such an amazing film. However, it was the height of the 1980s' shoulder pad craze and my, they are large. Although Elizabeth Perkins' character is defined by them, her shoulders get smaller as she gets softer. I think I learned a great lesson from the film... to ignore the fashion trends of the moment as they are fleeting. Create characters instead."

that, I do the research, and then I design the clothes. For me, that process pretty much stays that way every time. The projects that I enjoy most are those where I have a collaborative relationship with the hair and makeup team. **The Last Airbender** (2010) was amazingly fun and the one I'm designing now, **The Hunger Games** (2012), is fantastic. Before hair and makeup come on board a project, I do lots of research and create inspiration boards. Most people are not aware that it's about designing a total person, not just clothing. I'm designing a character from head to foot, and that includes hair and makeup. When hair and makeup arrive they give me even more ideas for the actors. That's how it should work.

On a contemporary film it can be difficult when movie stars come with their own hair and makeup people. It's very hard for a designer to interfere with that relationship. The designer's job is to make everybody happy, including us. Every different designer will produce a different costume from the same piece of research. It's an individual way of seeing things and a matter of taste. Maybe some designers are cleverer than others; definitely there are some way out there in the genius realm.

When I went to the interview for **A Little Princess** (1995), the director, Alfonso Cuarón, wanted to design the movie using all green. "What a challenge," I said. "Green can function →

> "Every director is different and they all work differently, although in a funny way the really good directors all have the same process."

like black and white; it's a cool color and a warm color at the same time." Apparently that got me the job, because nobody else liked green, even though I also told him, "I don't think you can do everything in green. You're in real buildings with wood stairs and in order to have the film look real, you will have to combine it with black and white. If the little girls wear green dresses, green stockings and green shoes it's too much of a cartoon. But if you have real black shoes and real black stockings with the green, that takes it out of the realm of comics."

Writer/director Gary Ross and I became friendly when he was the writer on **Big**. When he directed his first film, **Pleasantville** (1998), he remembered me and asked me to design it. When I read the script, it was such an incredible challenge to figure out how to work with black and white and color within the same film. Nobody really knew the technology, we all had to work it out together. There was no question that we could test fabrics and hair colors, but we didn't know if we were going to shoot the film entirely in color

and then turn it black and white or vice-versa. Eventually, we shot it in color and then de-saturated the film to black and white. Gary insisted that every frame be scrutinized to make sure that the shadows were right, the hair color, and the color of the dresses were right. Everything was done on the computer, frame by frame. Gary asked me to sit with Michael Southard, the color effects designer, to make sure that I approved every frame; it was so fascinating.

The Legend of Bagger Vance (2000) was directed by Robert Redford, a serious painter who went to the Paris Sorbonne University. When we first met we discussed the characters in the script, and we talked in terms of color palette when he was scouting locations on the golf course. After our conversation, I brought him some pages of American impressionist pictures in which the colors would be appropriate for the film. We had these great discussions about art and we never discussed individual garments; it was about the whole look of the film. To me, that's what designing is about. I'm creating a picture within a frame that

every person in the script has to be part of. We were in the prettiest locations in America with the nicest actors. It doesn't get better than that.

Whether a film is contemporary or period or a fantasy, I'm very particular about color palette control and always very aware that I'm framing a picture. Even on **The Hunger Games**, in which I have used more color than I've ever used in my entire life, it's a very controlled and tight palette. Otherwise, the screen becomes a mish-mash, like a bad painting. That's the only definable element that I can see in my work, although I'm sure other people may see something else.

It was a total fluke that I was hired to design **Harry Potter and the Sorcerer's Stone** (2001).

I went into the interview believing that they would never hire an American designer because the Harry Potter books are so English. Director Chris Columbus and producer David Heyman had interviewed a lot of designers who were much better known, including Americans, but I believe Warner Bros. liked me because of my work on **A Little Princess** and they recommended me. "Well, I'll just go and meet them so they know who I am, and that will be that," I thought. At the interview I was very open to many different ways to design the film and I was told I was the only designer who didn't scare Chris by having set-in-stone ideas. Still I was shocked when they called my agent the next day and said, "We want her."

J. K. Rowling and I met only once, with Chris and David, and it wasn't a long meeting. Basically, I brought some research pictures and asked questions about the characters in the books. "You talk about robes on Dumbledore. Are these the kind of robes you're talking about? And Madam Hooch, the flying instructor, to me she looks →

PLEASANTVILLE

(01–03) "It was a challenge to try to find the right balance between reality vs. stylization and not have people look silly. Joan Allen's costumes reflect her character's journey of self-knowledge. Her silhouette starts out with very large skirts **(01)** and then becomes deliberately more form fitting throughout the film **(03)**." Makovsky's beautiful illustration with fabric swatch for one of Betty's (played by Joan Allen) outfits **(01)** and as seen in the film **(02)**.

"Most people are not aware that it's about designing a total person, not just clothing. I'm designing a character from head to foot."

like the sort of gym teacher we all had that was a little mannish when we were in elementary school." And she said, "Yes, that's exactly right." J. K. didn't come around on a daily basis; she interfaced with Chris and the producers. Stuart Craig was the production designer and we worked very closely together.

Seabiscuit (2003) was one of those experiences that doesn't happen all that often. When I was hired I knew nothing about horseracing and I had to research the sport of horseracing and everyday life in the 1930s, including rich, middle-class and poor people's lives. I got to design everything, and everyone worked together very closely; I was very lucky to have great producers and a great crew. Gary Ross trusted that I knew what I was doing throughout the picture. I'd show him the pictures after the fittings and he made his comments, but essentially he trusts me to get on with it. The production designer was Jeannine Oppewall, who'd designed **Pleasantville**. It was a lot of hard work, but huge and amazing-looking.

Sometimes I get to design a contemporary film where I'm creating interesting characters, and make a lot of modern clothes, but it's not just "shopping." That was the case with **National Treasure** (2004) and the sequel, **National Treasure: Book of Secrets** (2007). They had mixed a little bit of historical stuff into the script and I traveled to places usually unavailable for shooting, like the national monuments and Library of Congress in Washington DC, and Philadelphia, and Mount Rushmore. How awesome is that?

The **National Treasure** movies used a lot of green screen technology, which luckily has changed. We don't have all the frustrating rules that we used to have about not using fabrics that shimmer, being careful of outlines and using no green in the costume. The costume would have to be pretty electric green to upset anything now in the camera. There's not only green screen, they are using blue screen, gray screen, and orange screen all for different things; it's amazing to me.

The most "out there" movies that I've ever designed are **The Hunger Games** and **X-Men:**

SEABISCUIT

(01–03) "My dream project. Creating many walks of life within a specific era. The challenge was to have new garments made and have them smoothly integrate with actual period footage and real period clothing." **(02)** Makovsky's illustration for Tobey Maguire as Red Pollard.

01

02

03

The Last Stand (2006), the third **X-Men** film. I'd never designed a comic-book movie before and even though I wasn't the one to create the franchise, it was my job to continue the look. Comic-book movies are harder to design than any other genre. Designers try to bring to life bizarre characters while dealing with so many opinions—from the creators of the comic book, the studio, the producers, directors, and actors on the film. And comic book costumes involve so many really difficult processes like sculpting and so many different film crafts—including CGI, to get those action hero suits to function properly.

My most challenging films were **The Hunger Games** and **Harry Potter**. Both these films are based on books with huge fan bases. Trying to get the director's vision and at the same time keep true to the essence of the book is terrifying for a designer. My resources on **The Hunger Games** were more limited than those on **Harry Potter** and it was a very large project. My terror is more about bringing a book to life on screen that millions of people have loved and whom I don't want to disappoint. What if I had designed Dumbledore wrong? People would hate me! I have to admit, I'm very proud that I designed the first **Harry Potter** movie and established those now legendary characters. **99**

THE LEGEND OF BAGGER VANCE
(04–06) "Really one of the best experiences of my career. The collaboration with Robert Redford and Stuart Craig was magical and what a lovely period. When sports clothing was truly glamorous." **(04)** Illustration of the cream hammered-satin dress made from a vintage piece of fabric Makovsky found, and how it appeared in the actual film as worn by Charlize Theron **(05)**.

Jean Louis

"It was back in 1935," Hollywood star Irene Dunne recalled, "I was walking past Hattie Carnegie's shop and saw this evening dress in the window. Hattie told me it was by a new designer who had just come from France." Born in Paris in 1907, Jean Louis studied fashion at the École des Arts Décoratifs. Dunne's purchase led to an extension on Jean Louis' work visa and the beginning of his career as a designer. Years later, another client, Joan Cohn, wife of Columbia Pictures president Harry Cohn, encouraged him to put Jean Louis under contract.

The first picture Jean Louis designed, **Together Again** (1944), starred his friend Irene Dunne. "Designing for films was a totally new experience for me," Louis admits, "the character was the important thing now. I couldn't dress Gilda as I would have dressed Rita Hayworth in her private life." He elaborates, "When you design for a film, you have to bear in mind that the costume has to be in accordance with the script and the character of the star, and who she plays." When Louis designed **You Gotta Stay**

Happy (1948) he observed, "You can't design exactly what fashion is doing at that moment." He continued, "We had that experience with Joan Fontaine. This was at about the time of the New Look from Dior. She wanted to have a dress like that and then the picture came out a year later and it was a catastrophe; the style had changed."

At Columbia, Jean Louis designed for a stable of Hollywood actresses and Rita Hayworth, who was Columbia's major star. Jean Louis' ravishing designs for Hayworth in **Gilda** (1946) made him famous. He says, "I tried to make everything for her very special, because it was also my chance to do special things." His ten pictures with Hayworth included Orson Welles' **The Lady from Shanghai** (1947) and **Pal Joey** (1957). Highlights of his work at Columbia include **Born Yesterday** (1950), **From Here to Eternity** (1953), **The Big Heat** (1953), and **The Solid Gold Cadillac** (1956), for which he won an Oscar.

After Harry Cohn died in 1958, "[Columbia] wanted to cut expenses," said Jean Louis. "If Harry Cohn was still living, I would still be there."

He was hired by producer Ross Hunter at Universal Studios to bring elegance to Doris Day, Sandra Dee, and Lana Turner. Doris Day remembered, "Ross Hunter hired Jean Louis to create my wardrobe and I adored everything he made for me. For the first time I was wearing clothes that I felt accentuated my body and enhanced the part I was playing." At Universal, Louis designed gowns for the stars in such classics as **Imitation of Life** (1959), **Pillow Talk** (1959), and **Thoroughly Modern Millie** (1967).

Jean Louis was also a popular freelance designer for Judy Garland in **A Star is Born** (with Irene Sharaff, 1954), Marilyn Monroe in **The Misfits** (1961), Marlene Dietrich in **Judgment at Nuremberg** (1961), and on television for **The Loretta Young Show** and Eva Gabor in **Green Acres**. In his 30-year career, Jean Louis designed for more than 180 films and received 14 Academy Award nominations.

03 The Thrill of it All (1963)

04 Gilda

04

03

Maurizio Millenotti

"Sometimes I start designing a costume with one idea and then I find an interesting textured cloth or a special detail that completely changes my mind about the dress. The clothes will also change with the actor who will wear them."

Born in Reggiolo, Italy, Maurizio Millenotti began his distinguished film career in the 1970s as an assistant to the legendary Piero Tosi and Gabriella Pescucci. The first film he designed was Sergio Corbucci's **My Darling, My Dearest** (1982), followed by **And the Ship Sails On** (1983) directed by fabled filmmaker Federico Fellini. Millenotti would later design Fellini's **The Voice of the Moon** (1990). For Franco Zeffirelli's adaptation of Verdi's opera **Otello** (1986), Millenotti and his co-designer Anna Anni received an Academy Award nomination.

Although he has primarily designed Italian films, he made his first English language film in Peter Greenaway's **The Belly of an Architect** (1987). His second film in English, Zeffirelli's **Hamlet** (1990), starring Mel Gibson, earned Millenotti a second Academy Award nomination. His magnificent costumes on **Hamlet** were not forgotten by Gibson, who later hired Millenotti to design the controversial **The Passion of the Christ** (2004). He designed two films for Giuseppe Tornatore, **Malèna** (2000) and **The Legend of 1900** (1998), both set in the 1940s. Millenotti's designs enhanced Oscar Wilde's classic farce, **The Importance of Being Earnest** (2002), and medieval romance **Tristan + Isolde** (2006), the story of the original star-crossed lovers.

Maurizio Millenotti continues to enjoy an illustrious career in film, while lending his talents to the ballet, theater and opera at acclaimed institutions such as Rome's Teatro dell'Opera and Milan's Teatro alla Scala. His most recent films include **The Nativity Story** (2006) for director Catherine Hardwicke, **Parlami d'amore** (2008) and **Un Altro Mondo** (2010)—both directed by Silvio Muccino—and **The Cardboard Village** (2011) by Ermanno Olmi.

Maurizio Millenotti

" My career in costume design all happened very much by chance, because I had been raised and programmed for another job. As the son of an Italian motocross champion, I was meant to pursue a similar career to my father's—automobiles, garages, and car repair—and much to my chagrin because I had completely different ideas about my path in life. I did try to make it work, but I gave it up once I realized that I would never be able to see it through successfully as a career.

My love of costuming started with my passion for cinema. I was born in a small village in Emilia, Reggiolo, in a village between Mantova and Reggio Emilia. In the 1950s, they showed all the big MGM movies at our cinema. For us kids, they were an utter marvel. I would spend all my time watching Hollywood movies and was enchanted by that world of adventure and lavishness. I adored "hero" films such as **Knights of the Round Table** (1953, costumes designed by Roger Furse), **Ivanhoe** (1952, costumes designed by Roger Furse), and the great westerns. I was taken by period pieces like **The Three Musketeers** (1948, costumes designed by Walter Plunkett); I probably saw it hundreds of times. When I went to see **Quo Vadis** (1951, costumes designed by Herschel McCoy) my family had to pull me from the theater. I had stayed in the theater for hours, having spent the entire afternoon from the first show late into the evening. My family was desperate; they couldn't get me away from the movies. Even as a child, I was overwhelmed with that imagery.

After my obligatory Italian military service, at 19 years old, I went to Paris. From that point everything in my life and career happened by chance. I became friends with some painters that worked for a stage lab called "Hector" where they created masks and props. At that time, they were doing a stage show for artist and costume designer Leonor Fini. I was delighted by the work. The moment that I helped them on the show I realized that this was a world that might suit me permanently. As soon as I got back to Italy I tried to make contacts in the theater and

immediately started working at a "fabbrica di confezioni" [a tailor shop creating dresses] in Milan. Coincidentally, my family used to buy wine from the brother of Umberto Tirelli [owner of Tirelli Costumi, the famous costume house in Rome], who used to live in Gualtieri, a village close to mine. One day he said, "Hey, I could introduce you to my brother if you'd like!"

Tirelli offered me work as an unpaid trainee, but I could not afford to take that opportunity. However, two months later Tirelli needed a replacement for someone from his staff and I had the job. It was as if I'd been struck by lightning. I went for a test period (three days) from Milan to Rome, and the first person I met at Tirelli was the costume designer Piero Tosi who was designing **La caduta degli dei** (**The Damned**, 1969). All the best designers of the Italian and international movie industry came to Tirelli. I immediately resigned from my position in Milan and moved to Rome. Rome and Tirelli Costumi provided a real costume design school and they were my university. I was there for three and a half years and that's where my passion for costumes actually started. The love of the cinema already existed, but that's where I was able to develop my skill as a costume designer.

Although there were many mentors in my life, Tirelli gave me the chance of a lifetime. Like so many designers, I was deeply impressed by the work of Tosi and the great costume designer Lila De Nobili who designed for the theater and the opera. I remember finding the costumes that Lila De Nobili had made for **The Merchant of Venice**, a famous stage version directed by Ettore Giannini. Inspired by Rembrandt, the textures and the colors of these costumes really oozed "the art of painting" and the magic of his portraits. I would watch all these distinguished designers for hours, almost trying to dissect and define their creative process.

At first, I was an assistant in Tirelli's tailor shop. Then, I learned how to dye textiles and I was assigned to many different departments at the costume house and was able to learn a bit of everything else. After some time, I started to

> "A designer has many sources for inspiration that change from project to project. The inspiration must also come from the relationship that's struck between a script and the director."

think about the creative possibilities that might exist for me outside Tirelli. I accepted a job as a fashion designer, making dresses for a few boutiques in Rome. It took just three or four months of doing this to figure out that I wanted nothing to do with fashion. Fashion has its specific commercial needs that are quite different to those of costume. In cinema and the theater, a costume designer works on a story; we are dressing an actor playing a character. Fashion is completely different in that they must dress the everyday woman, the bourgeoisie who shops. The very idea of understanding a commercial

market was not something that suited me and not something that I enjoyed. So, at the very first opportunity, I decided to return to costume design. At the time, Lucia Mirisola, the wife of director Luigi Magni, was designing costumes and she generously allowed me to become her assistant. That first position started my professional career as an assistant designer, which was followed most notably as assistant designer to Gabriella Pescucci. From that point, I was at last involved in this fabled movie industry that included the great directors Mauro Bolognini, Patroni Griffi, and Francesco Rosi. →

ANNA KARENINA

(01–02) "This film was shot on real locations in St. Petersburg and Moscow. The inspiration for these clothes came from photographs of the Russian aristocracy. I tried to recreate the richness and the elegance of those days before the revolution. For the costumes of the peasants I found some fantastic references in an ethnic museum in St. Petersburg, a fantastic museum unique in all the world."

> "In cinema and the theater, a costume designer works on a story; we are dressing an actor playing a character."

My beacon and main inspiration as a designer was Piero Tosi, but I also feel that an artist needs to relieve himself from the pressure of role models. A designer has many sources for inspiration that change from project to project. The inspiration must also come from the relationship that's struck between a script and the director. It's up to the director to communicate his unique vision to the costume designer. Fellini's world was very different from Zeffirelli's, each man placed certain demands on their designers and other directors have their own style.

The creative process is pretty much the same for all designers. The work always begins chronologically, meeting the director, reading the screenplay, then researching and discussing the story with the director. The research is now so much easier on the internet and I can even dig up stuff online that once was lost. When I started in the business, I would go to libraries, which may have provided a much deeper search, because I'd spend entire days and be rewarded with unexpected finds. After research I begin the real preparation. I am not good at drawing but I can express and clearly communicate my idea to a maker. There are period movies where I provided no drawings at all, like on **Anna Karenina** (1997). I worked from authentic period dresses by recreating them with similar fabric, cut and the trim. If needed, I use a costume illustrator who works under my guidance and I work with them very closely. Often, a costume may change when it is placed on the dress form for the first time. Sometimes I start designing a costume with one idea and then I find an interesting textured cloth or a special detail that completely changes my mind about the dress. The clothes will also change with the actor who will wear them. I am not someone who'll impose a costume on an actor. After all, I don't design for mannequins or marble statues —actors are people!

How involved the director wants to be in the development of the costume always depends on the individual director and the project. There are directors that I have worked with who only want to see the finished product on the set. In my experience, American directors are not really interested in the development of the costumes from script to screen. I give them some ideas about the character and then they more or less trust me. Italian directors seem to have other expectations from a designer. Fellini wanted

THE LEGEND OF 1900

(01) "This was a very hard movie for costume, first, because it took place on a ship and also because I used real vintage pieces combined with my designs for four decades of costumes for different seasons and social classes. There were costumes from the lower classes to the aristocracy with lots of special characters from 1900 to 1930."

to know everything. He'd come to the shop to see the fabric, to try things on, to have conversations about the script and the character. Director Giuseppe Tornatore was very meticulous on some details; he's demanding, but also trusting. He was especially exacting on **Malèna** (2000), which was about his own Sicily, his world, his land. It seems that American filmmakers have been taught that everyone has his own role on a production—the director, costume designer, production designer—under the guidance of a producer. There are exceptions, of course; the directors with whom I've worked were easy and appreciative collaborators.

The first film that I designed was Fellini's **E la nave va** (**And the Ship Sails On**, 1983), and it was the most challenging. I felt totally inadequate; that's when I started losing my hair! At first, working with Fellini was scary, but as it went on it became a wonderful experience. I'd already met Fellini when I was Gabriella Pescucci's assistant on **La Città delle donne** (**City of Women**, 1980). After that, he asked me to design. He'd call me on the phone and I wouldn't answer. Then I got a very firm phone call, "I want to see you! Come!" Fellini asked me to collect research for a film that was set in 1914, and he wanted to be very precise. I traveled to all the great Italian theaters looking for documentation, and I found much that Fellini was looking for about the singers and characters from the era. **And the Ship Sails On** was an extraordinary experience; we shot on sets that were mounted on gear that could change the way a ship moves over waves. We had a fake sea. Never before had I experienced emotions as strong as those Fellini could create on a set. Fellini's rages were unforgettable although they would never last long. He was Jupiter personified, shooting lightning.

Fellini was very important in my life and we loved each other very much. He'd call me every once in a while with an idea and I'd run over to see him. In addition to designing the costumes for his last film, **La voce della Luna** (1990), we also made quite a few commercials together, one with a very young Anna Falchi. He was →

(02) "For **Malèna** I had to rebuild the post World War II atmosphere and it wasn't easy, especially because we shot the film in color, but we are used to seeing that period from Italian neo-realism, in black and white. To make the costumes believable I used clothes from the 1940s and dyed them all other colors, then mended and transformed them to give the impression of the poverty and the human desperation of that period. Monica Bellucci had so many changes—from a middle-class woman, she then loses everything and we had to make all those transformations."

02

Allowing the imagination to run free

(01–02) "For **Tristan + Isolde** (2006), there was absolutely no research in the period and no reference for original clothes. The costumes ended up being much closer to my fantasy of the clothes that existed at that time. When I am freer to create, my creative process happens gradually. This always depends on a sudden moment of incredible creativity and on the opportunities that arise. Designing and making costumes for period and fantasy films allows me to be much more imaginative with my design."

THE NATIVITY STORY

(03–05) "**The Nativity Story** came after **The Passion of the Christ**, was the same period and shot at the same locations, but I tried to tell a different story through the costumes. Nativity is more joyful and I used light colors and found inspiration from the beautiful landscape around us. As often happens in the movies, many of the costumes that I designed did not make it to the final cut." Illustrations showing Millenotti's costume designs for the film (04–05).

THE PASSION OF THE CHRIST

(06–08) "Mel Gibson had a very clear vision of the look of the movie and he guided me while at the same time giving me complete creative freedom. It was a very difficult world to recreate because there was no visual reference for the Palestinian common people and of life in ancient Palestine. I started reading books and studying how fabrics were made at that time and tried to understand the colors and how they prepared the dyes. **The Passion of the Christ** was a hard movie to make with a very short preparation time, and my God, I had to dress Jesus Christ!" Illustrations showing Millenotti's costume designs for the film **(07–08)**.

THE IMPORTANCE OF BEING EARNEST

(01–03) "We made all Rupert Everett's and Colin Firth's costumes in Italy, which was scandalous for the English, but the results are quite good (01)." Illustrations showing Millenotti's costume designs for the film (02–03).

"Fellini wanted to know everything. He'd come to the shop to see fabric…to have conversations about the script and the character."

very enthusiastic and kept saying, "Have you seen her? She's Finnish!" He'd say "Finnish," as if it was something really exotic.

It was such a pleasure to dress Monica Bellucci for **Malèna**; I loved watching all her transformations. Piero Tosi told me it was one of the few films about the 1940s where he felt that the costumes were believable, a great compliment. It's hard to make films about the 1940s in color, because we're used to seeing them in black and white. In Italy, we are so used to our neo-realistic films of the post-war era. Another film that was very hard to make was Tornatore's **La leggenda del pianista sull'oceano (The Legend of 1900**, 1998), which took place across many eras and actually ended in the 1940s. Although there was plenty of money for the production budget, I got very little money to design the costumes, but the film turned out well.

Working with director Franco Zeffirelli was a major professional collaboration. **Hamlet** (1990) was a unique experience for me because the production was based in London and we had to create everything from there. This decision was not without its problems, because a bunch of Italians and an Australian who was designing **Hamlet** was somewhat offensive to the English costumers. After three weeks of unhappy pre-production Zeffirelli asked me to replace the costume designer that Mel Gibson had initially requested. Later, when I designed **The Importance of Being Earnest** (2002) in London, the tension with the Brits happened once again. The idea that an Italian would go to Italy to make costumes for Oscar Wilde was sacrilegious. For whatever reason, I regret to say that they really gave me a hard time. For Zeffirelli's **Otello** (1986) my inspiration was the Venetian paintings of the middle 1500s—Tintoretto, Tiziano and most of all Veronese. We had the wonderful soprano-turned-actress Katia Ricciarelli, who was perfect to play Desdemona. She really looked like someone straight out of a Veronese painting.

I've had the opportunity to design quite a few modern movies like Peter Greenaway's **The**

Belly of an Architect (1987). Bertolucci once called me to ask, "Hey, what's this **Amici ahrarara** (2001)?" I switch genres whenever possible, and **Amici ahrarara** was a comedy. I designed it mostly because I needed to pay the rent, but also to develop a relationship with a producer. There are many other reasons to take a job than working with a great director. I like to be able to keep my assistants and my crew working, who may be unemployed or between jobs—that's another reason for me to take two movies at the same time. When I look back on some of the modern films I have designed, while I am designing the film I hate it, but as time goes by I can look back on my work more generously.

A costume designer has to understand the needs of each director and each project because each project is unique. Designers need imagination and although it's tough, the ability to understand different points of view. I was fortunate enough to work in the great moviemaking industry of the 1970s, the last gasp of great cinema in an era when they made 300 films per year in Italy. You could choose to work on whatever movie you liked and be chosen even if you were an assistant. The business has all changed so much. The pre-production time has changed with at most four to five weeks of pre-production. A designer must be quick to get it all done. It's not possible to do deeper research; it's all about a specific effect on screen. Sadly, quality is the least important item. Of course, it was all very different for Fellini's films. **"**

Ellen Mirojnick

"There's a new word: mashup. That's what I am, a mashup designer, a collagist, and I always have been from the beginning. It comes from my art background."

Growing up in New York City, Ellen Mirojnick studied photography at the School of Visual Arts before enrolling in Parsons School of Design. She didn't stay long. Talented and ambitious, Mirojnick soon scouted fashion trends for the Federated Department Stores and at an early age became a ready-to-wear fashion designer. In the late 1970s she designed her first film, the racy **French Quarter** (1978), which she followed by assisting costume designer Kristi Zea on the musical **Fame** (1980), and the romance **Endless Love** (1981).

Mirojnick has designed three films for director Adrian Lyne, beginning with the box office hit **Fatal Attraction** (1987), which also marked her first production with actor Michael Douglas. She has designed 13 other films starring Douglas, including Paul Verhoeven's now classic **Basic Instinct** (1992), **The Ghost and the Darkness** (1996), and **A Perfect Murder** (1998). Mirojnick's luxurious threads and suspenders for the ruthless tycoon Gordon Gekko for the emblematic **Wall Street** (1987) transformed corporate menswear; 20 years later she redefined the look for the sequel, **Wall Street: Money Never Sleeps** (2010).

Best known for her sublime work on contemporary films such as **Cocktail** (1988), Mirojnick has proven herself in every genre. She received a BAFTA Award nomination in 1993 for Richard Attenborough's **Chaplin** (1992), co-designed with British designer John Mollo. In the 1990s, she designed the action classic **Speed** (1994); the sexually explicit **Showgirls** (1995); the neo-noir **Mulholland Falls** (1996); and the sci-fi adventure **Starship Troopers** (1997). Recently she tackled **Unfaithful** (2002), the monster flick, **Cloverfield** (2008), and **G.I. Joe: The Rise of Cobra** (2009).

Ellen Mirojnick

" In 1955 or 1956, when I was in the first grade, I'm proud to say I was in the first group of New York City children bused to a black school. My family lived in a predominantly Jewish, middle-class white neighborhood in the Bronx. My great-grandfather was a painter, a fine artist, but he earned his living as a tailor. When I was four or five, I started to paint and I did it very, very easily. Later I wanted to be a singer, but my teachers said I was tone deaf. My mom was very protective, she didn't know what she was protecting—I was like another species—but she didn't want to mess with it. After I graduated from the High School of Music and Art, I wanted to go to the San Francisco Art Institute, to study fine arts. It was 1967 and Haight-Ashbury was in its prime. My dad had traveled around the United States and was aware of this. Even though I was no hippie or flower child, my dad said, "You're not going to Sin City."

Instead, I went to the School of Visual Arts in Manhattan, where I was fortunate to study with Chuck Close. He taught the equivalent of 3D design for photography. One of my favorite assignments was to create "your own" *Life* magazine. Plexiglas was big at the time and I built this three-dimensional, freeform *Life* magazine with images roaming throughout. Jack Potter, my teacher, was my master; he was the one who taught me how to see. To this day, I would say he is the single most influential person in my life.

I dropped out of SVA and later went to Parsons School for Design and studied fashion. The first year was draping. The teacher said, "I'm going to drape the dummy and mark the fabric. I want you to take it home and sew it, and then we're going to put it back on the dummy." My fabric never fit the form the next day, which confounded the teacher. I could design all day long and paint beautiful pictures, but I couldn't sew. I could not get that small motor skill down, so Parsons asked me to leave.

While I was in school I'd work with my Aunt Sandra at night, making funky jewelry. Through her I'd met Bernie Ozer, who was the head of Federated Department Stores. What he said

"went" in the junior sportswear market. After Parsons asked me to leave, I went to Bernie and asked if he could get me a job in one of his companies. "Before I recommend, I want to see what you can do," he told me, and he tested me. "Go to the street and find me four trends." Once I'd sussed out the situation on the street I'd come back and tell Bernie, "Girls are wearing shorts with platform shoes and little white anklets"—or pea coats or whatever. "You're the girl," he said.

He recommended me to a ready-to-wear company called Happy Legs that offered me my own line. After a while, I fell in love with the man who became my husband, and then worked at Happy Legs as the head designer until 1976 or '77. The company went from nothing to $60 million annually, a lot of money in those days. Herb Schneiderman, one of the owners, was

01 Mirojnick's costume designs for **Chaplin** earned her a BAFTA Award nomination

02 Glenn Close as Alex Forrest in the psychological thriller **Fatal Attraction**

another important mentor. He taught me how to work with people, how to be myself and how not to compromise about my gut feelings, while still paying attention to others, to business, and to what sells. What mattered most to Herb was to communicate effectively. It helped that I could identify and initiate a trend, because that meant money to the company. In addition, at Happy Legs I learned how to run a workroom and to design wearable clothes. But if I told my assistant, "Let me show you how I want it," she'd say, "Stay away from the dummy. Just draw me a picture!"

My husband was working on an independent film in New Orleans, a period piece called **French Quarter** (1978). I hadn't had a vacation, so I went to New Orleans to visit. They needed a costume designer and asked me if I would design it. It was the most exciting offer I'd ever had. I'd always loved the movies, I thought they were magic. When I said, "I don't sew," they said, "That's okay. We don't have anyone else. You have to design it." Herb let me design it, provided that I return to New York and put in seven weeks' worth of work at the company. The costume budget was, like, a dollar. The costume house, Brooks Van Horn in New York, agreed to let me rent whatever I wanted. Then I wound up being the costume supervisor as well and I don't know how I did it; with the sewing and pins, I had holes in my fingers, but I did it with a big smile and loved it. The finished film wound up, I think, in drive-ins. After that, Herb said, "I don't want you to freelance costume design without a job. Work here at Happy Legs while you integrate into the film community." He was absolutely fabulous.

One of the fellows on **French Quarter** was a commercial assistant director and introduced me to a production house called Myers & Griner/Cuesta, where costume and production designer Kristi Zea also worked. When **Fame** (1980) came along, she was asked to design the clothes and she hired me as her assistant. That was the beginning of my costume design career. Kristi designed the principal actors and I helped design all the rest. After that we collaborated again on **Endless Love** (1981). →

"Costume design is the most misunderstood category in the film industry. No one realizes the contribution the costume designer makes to the whole movie."

I loved old films, film noir and the glitz of the 1930s' musicals and I studied up on film, costumes and their influence on fashion. I wasn't aware of the contribution of the costume designer then and no particular designer directly inspired me. When I was young, I saw Edith Head on TV on the **Art Linkletter Show**. She was this cute little lady with bangs and glasses, and she talked about costume, fashion, and how to improve your image. In 1990, I moved to California, got in the Costume Designers Guild and finally became a "Hollywood" costume designer myself.

My design process is the same on every movie and it starts deep within me. The goal is to figure out what I need creatively to bring to the table. First I break down the script, going for an overview of the story and trying to understand the director's vision. And then I have the same conversation with the production designer and cinematographer. Next, I do my research to see if there's something out there I can use or if I have to make it all up. Ultimately, everything becomes clear and there is a free flow of ideas. Depending on the project, the research will either be extensive or not; there's no set pattern. From the beginning of my career, I have learned to trust my instincts. Then I get ready to work with the actors to create the characters.

The director is the key to the movie and I take the director's vision and translate it into three-dimensional characters. Unfortunately, these days directors sometimes seem to be facilitators of somebody else's vision, perhaps the producer or the studio or whoever's funding the picture. On **G.I. Joe: The Rise of Cobra** (2009) there was the studio, the producers and the director, Stephen Sommers, who wanted to make a James Bond film, and then there was the toy company, Hasbro. My job was to reinterpret the franchise, refresh the toys and make them cool, and to create new iconic images that would sell. I had to design it all really fast, so we could start shooting before the writers' strike began.

To be honest, I didn't know what I was doing. For the first time, I worked with costume illustrators, creating camouflage fabric that incorporated G.I. Joe in the design and learning about liquid armor and military gear. At one point I asked Stephen, "Do you want that super-hero look?" He did. "Can you put the muscles on the outside of the suits?" he asked. "Hmm," I said, "I'll get right back to you." I looked at video games and worked with the illustrators. I didn't know that we were illustrating the characters to sell the movie to the brand.

01–02 The Chronicles of Riddick

Studies for Jacob's Ladder

(03–04) "Adrian Lyne found a photograph titled 'Leo' taken by Joel-Peter Witkin. The image inspired the film's horrific 'Vibrating Man.' During pre-production he was uncomfortable making a commitment to visual effects, but he wanted to create a collection of images that were as haunting as the photo, to be used throughout the film. Makeup artist, Richard Dean, and I decided to experiment with practical solutions. Using an actor, and combinations of makeup, water, a few props, and different fabrics, these photos captured what Adrian was looking for. This experiment became the vocabulary that underscores the disturbing imagery of the film."

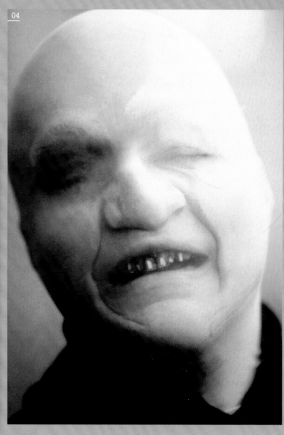

We worked and worked, and Hasbro was happy to have some new toys to market. We sold the movie and then we had to make it.

There's a new word: mashup. That's what I am, a mashup designer, a collagist, and I always have been from the beginning. It comes from my art background. I take from every source imaginable, whether it is something visual that exists or a fabric, color, texture, form, architecture, and mash it all up in broad strokes. My design is architectural; I strip it clean, I don't focus on fine details. My sensibility and my eye want to see the character clearly, to enhance the character, to tell the story in its cleanest form. The end result is simple and sleek, and polished, using collage to get to the architecture of the human form. I don't think I've ever done a fussy costume in my life. Mostly I've designed contemporary film and sci-fi, and contemporary costume is my favorite category. I find the present fascinating and I love documenting the time we live in, all the different characters and their stories. Still, I'd like to design a period film, something decorative like **Marie Antoinette**. It would be a challenge not strip away any of the style that really defines that period.

Fatal Attraction (1987) was a great psychological thriller. I loved it, I loved creating those characters—and it was a brilliant movie. It was my first with Michael Douglas, my first →

> "My design is architectural; I strip it clean, I don't focus on fine details. My sensibility and my eye want to see the character clearly, to enhance the character."

with Adrian Lyne, and my first movie with [producers] Stanley Jaffe and Sherry Lansing. Jaffe and Lyne had interviewed every costumer designer in New York and I was the last one. No one knew me; I'd only designed two movies, and they said, "Come in." Adrian liked me because I designed a couple of commercials; I was a bad bet, but that's why I really got the job. My first meeting with Stanley and Adrian, I brought some tear sheets and some design ideas for the principal actors. I said, "When Glenn Close's character goes to the parking garage to get revenge on him [Michael Douglas] and he comes in with the rabbit, I think that she should be wearing a beautiful coat and…she's not going to wear anything underneath it. She's only going to wear high heels, a beautiful coat and maybe some undies." Well these two guys fell down and went to heaven. They said, "Who's this girl? Oh great! She gets it." The psychological study of **Fatal Attraction** was absolutely brilliant.

Wall Street (1987) is the most influential film on my resume, not only in the cinematic world, but in what it meant to men's power dressing. Gordon Gekko became iconic; he was synonymous with how those men dressed in the world. His name became a verb—to be Gekkoed. He defined that decade. That's not what I set out to do, but that's what it became.

Wall Street: Money Never Sleeps (2010) was the hardest design challenge I've faced in 25 years of designing, because Gordon was such a big question mark. Who had he become in the 20 years since the first movie? What did he look like? And what would Michael Douglas bring to the table? Michael and I had worked together on 12 movies. I played around with some ideas that would not have been correct. I didn't know the right answer until director Oliver Stone asked me, "Is he going to have a better suit than Shia LaBeouf?" And I realized the answer was "No." And, amazingly, after creating this monster in

01–02 **Showgirls**. Illustration by Lois DeArmond

01

02

G.I. JOE: THE RISE OF COBRA

(03–06) "It seemed ludicrous at the time to cast Sienna Miller, an adorable blonde with a bohemian vibe, as the fierce, dark and sultry villain. I began by determining what I needed to build to give her a voluptuous shape. At 5′4″ she needed height to be commanding and six-inch heels were the answer. Many different tones of raven-haired wigs later I was confident that Sienna would become 'The Baroness' **(05)**. Her partner, Storm Shadow (Byung-hun Lee, a Korean superstar) arrived in LA. Byung-hun didn't know that he was the villain and didn't think he was in good enough shape to show his body. He didn't want to cover his face, didn't fully understand English, and told me that Korean's don't wear white! **(06)**" Illustrations by Christian Cordella **(03–04)**.

my head, it didn't matter. It was interesting to be involved with Gordon again and it was a great visual exercise for me to come back to that character. Gordon Gekko still lived.

The Chronicles of Riddick (2004) presented another kind of challenge. At the first meeting the walls were filled with illustrations and storyboards, beautiful drawings and not a space in between. "What's the problem?" I said. "This movie's designed already." The problem was that it was ugly and my job was to fix it. Sometimes the budget is the problem, like on **Cloverfield** (2008), where there was no money. But I jumped in, and it was very hard work, but it was fun. →

My favorite movie was **Jacob's Ladder** (1990), about a postal worker in 1970s' New York who is losing his grip on reality. Director Adrian Lyne gave Richard Dean, the brilliant makeup artist, and me the task of creating really scary, psychologically challenging imagery. We created things never before seen in the visual effects world—gritty, really sick, and crazy. **Jacob's Ladder**, I would say, is the psychological thriller/ horror movie of all time. People use it as a reference now when they want to create a very dark world.

Some people make footprints on your heart and they never leave your life and that was how I felt about director Paul Verhoeven. We started **Basic Instinct** (1992) and Sharon Stone was meant to be the devil. I was told by Paul Verhoeven, "She's the devil, and you have to control her," and I said, "Okay, thanks." We went out to lunch and then I took her to the first fitting, and we had created the beginnings of a wardrobe for her, a closet for her, just to see what she was like. She walked into the fitting room at Bill Hargate Costumes and cried. She took me into the room next door and said, "I'm sorry, I can't go in the room," and I said, "Why?" and she said, "I've never seen more beautiful clothes in my life and I think that somebody's going to come and tell me that the jig is up and Michelle Pfeiffer's going to come in and put those clothes on." I said, "Well, no, this is all for you. I'll hold your hand through it, but we have to do the fitting," and she said, "Okay," and she did, and she sent me flowers the next day.

Costume design is the most misunderstood category in the film industry. No one realizes the contribution the costume designer makes to the whole movie. When I started I asked myself, "What job can I do? How can I be part of the movie business?" Costume design was the answer. There was a natural progression from what I was designing in ready-to-wear to costuming. If I was at the same crossroads today, 30 years later, I might have wanted to be a director. 🙶

WALL STREET: MONEY NEVER SLEEPS (03–07) "This is a world where at first glance everyone appears the same. However, the choice of fabric, the cut of the suit, the shape and color of the shirt, the size of the collar, tie or no tie, and the accessories, reveal, individualize, and inform the character. 'Tonic Blue' is the color of a shark's underbelly. That color combined with the luxuriousness of a silk and cashmere fabrication was perfect to bring the shark king Gordon Gekko (Michael Douglas) back to life **(05,** illustration by Sara O'Donnell). Jake (Shia LaBeouf) would embody the newness of 'stealth wealth.' I chose the hard hand of cool, gray mohair to create a perfectly tailored suit. By adding height and depth to the collar of his crisp white shirt, he would have a stronger jaw line. When everything came together it felt as if he was a super-hero **(07)**." Mirojnick created mood boards to inspire her **(03–04)**. Carey Mulligan as Winnie Gekko **(06)**.

01–02 Mirojnick's threads and suspenders for tycoon Gordon Gekko in **Wall Street** transformed corporate menswear in the late 1980s

Aggie Guerard Rodgers

"I am there to help paint a picture.
I don't design fashion. My goal is for
the people in the story to be real."

Aggie Guerard Rodgers earned a bachelor's degree in Theater Arts from California State University Fresno, worked for the American Conservatory Theater and got an MFA in Costume Design, before she was hired to design George Lucas's classic tale of California adolescence, **American Graffiti** (1973). During that interview she recalled "dragging the main" in her sister's cherry/blue '54 Ford, and instantly the job was hers.

Raised in San Francisco, she became a frequent collaborator of many Bay Area filmmakers. Her second film was Francis Ford Coppola's ground-breaking **The Conversation** (1974). She re-teamed with George Lucas on the third installment of his **Star Wars** saga, **Star Wars: Episode VI—Return of the Jedi** (1983, directed by Richard Marquand) and her costumes, including Princess Leia's crowd-pleasing tiny metal bikini, won her a Saturn Award. Rodgers also designed Philip Kaufman's update of the horror classic, **Invasion of the Body Snatchers** (1978).

In 1975 Rodgers designed Milos Forman's Academy Award-winning film adaptation of Ken Kesey's novel, **One Flew Over the Cuckoo's Nest**. Her sly sense of humor is evident in **Pee-wee's Big Adventure** (1985) and the witty **Beetlejuice** (1988), both directed by master of the gothic, Tim Burton. Her authentic period clothes for Steven Spielberg's **The Color Purple** (1985) earned Rodgers an Academy Award nomination. The quirky charm of **Benny & Joon** (1993) starring Johnny Depp was followed by **The Fugitive** (1993), and Norman Jewison's gritty **The Hurricane** (1999), starring Denzel Washington as wrongly imprisoned, middleweight boxer Rubin Carter. In 2005, Rodgers lent her design talents to Chris Columbus' film of Jonathan Larson's Pulitzer Prize-winning musical **Rent**.

Aggie Guerard Rodgers

" My mom was a milliner for a small theater when I was growing up in Fresno, California. She collected a lot of millinery blocks and designed some hats for a theater group, but she didn't like the timetables and was often late in delivering them. We had a very small house and it was packed with shelves of feathers, trim and all kinds of horsehair. My mom had such fun with her millinery that it made me want to get into this madness of theater. So much so, that after I received a BA in theater arts from California State College at Fresno, I applied to the American Conservatory Theater in San Francisco, and I was hired as their shopper for two seasons. Ann Roth was one of the distinguished guest costume designers, as well as Anthony Powell and Lewis Brown. The theater group did 27 shows in two theaters in two seasons. I left exhausted and went back to school for my Master's degree at Cal State, Long Beach.

Upon graduation, I returned to San Francisco and interviewed for **American Graffiti** (1973). When I told the unit production manager, Jimmy [James] Hogan, that I'd never designed a movie he looked at me like I was crazy. "Why do you think you can do it?" he asked. "I don't really know," I answered. "How old are you?" I told him. He asked where I grew up. He asked, "Do you know anything about dragging the main?" "Yes," I said. "My sister had a '54 Ford with the door handles taken off." He stood up from his chair and went and got George Lucas. George talked to me for a few minutes and gave me the job; I was the ninth person they saw and I never left the office.

My costume budget was $2,000 and there wasn't even a costume set person to dress the actors. Except for one sweater that came from a friend of George's, all the clothes came from secondhand stores, which made a huge difference to how the film looked. The clothes just looked like they were real and not made for the film. When it came to the prom scene I was allowed to bring in two crew members to help dress the extras for the prom dance. Despite all these difficulties, I never had so much fun in my

01 Kim Basinger as Celeste Martin in **My Stepmother is an Alien**

life. Francis Ford Coppola was the executive producer and after **American Graffiti** he hired me for **The Conversation** (1974). I have had the luck to do two more films for him and there were times where I sat with Francis as he told the actor who the character was. I was there to hear the same words that the actor heard; that's fabulous for a designer.

When I started out working with Francis Ford Coppola on **The Conversation**, his producer, Fred Roos, gave me a cupboard in the Cinemobile—a large bus that carried all the equipment for lighting and camera—to hang all of Gene Hackman's clothes. When I designed **Rent** (2005), I had two 40-foot trailers filled with clothes for the film. An amazing difference in 30 years! In the early 1970s, I designed a little film in Los Angeles at the old MGM studios. It was my →

04 Cocoon

05 Johnny Depp and Mary Stuart Masterson in **Benny & Joon**

"Films should not look like television where the costumes are all ironed before the next shot. I'm very interested in the common man."

Not letting a limited budget stand in your way

(02–03) **American Graffiti:** "I scoured the Goodwill shops in San Francisco for petticoats and saddle oxford shoes, but I couldn't find Lantz dresses. I called my mother in Fresno and she found the Capezio shoes and this dress (50 cents at Goodwill) that I put on Candy Clark (03). My sister and her friends had worn this type of shoe in high school in Fresno and I based a lot of the costumes on what my sister and her friends wore at that time." (02) Ron Howard as Steve and Cindy Williams as Laurie.

first studio film and the lot was filled with lots of things that are no longer there, like the swimming pools for Esther Williams! But one of the many things I remember that helped us so much was being able to take the laundry into the costume department at the end of the day of filming and have the actor's nylons and lingerie washed overnight by a shop employee, and that's all they did, the laundry. The studios supplied the costume department with wonderful services, like the dyeing of fabric overnight and staffing a complete tailor shop. They were very generous.

I had a really interesting beginning to my career. You interact with the most interesting actors, directors and production designers, and try to make each project look great (or not so great). When I finished **The Conversation**, I worked as a set costumer on the TV show **The Streets of San Francisco** (1972), starring Michael Douglas. I wanted to see if the Los Angeles costumers did things differently than we did in San Francisco. Luckily for me Douglas later hired me to design **One Flew Over the Cuckoo's Nest** (1975). After these three successful films I was on my way.

I do worry about young designers who try to satisfy everyone. We want the film to look appropriate to the script. We work for the project and the director. I'm not working to keep an actor on the pages of style magazines. It's not my concern. What does the character look like? That is my biggest concern. I know that sometimes directors and producers think we are there to shop, but I am really there to help them paint their picture. I don't design fashion. My goal is for the people in the story to be real, even if they're in **Beetlejuice** (1988). They may be nuts, but they are also real.

I've found that there's one shop for every character when I'm designing modern films. I think I scared Tim Burton a little bit on **Beetlejuice** because I took him to this upscale boutique in Los Angeles called Maxfield Bleu. Tim personally was still wearing a lot of clothes from the Goodwill. When we went into Maxfield's, some of the shirts were $600 and $700 each. I

01–02 Beetlejuice

think it made him kind of nervous that I would spend so much for a shirt. Maybe it was nuts to take him there, but at least he knew what was coming. I said, "I really think most of the mother's and father's clothes are in this store. It's going to be great looking." I did have the red wedding dress made in downtown LA in a Mexican bridal shop, but aside from that, we made a lot of clothes, and then we went to Maxfield's.

For **Something to Talk About** (1995) with Julia Roberts, I didn't make or shop for things in Los

> "I had a wonderful illustrator from the art department who would sit in the office next to mine drawing, which was great because I don't draw."

Angeles to ship to the South. Instead, I went on location a few weeks early, shopped regionally and found the stores where Southern women shop. The clothes in **Something to Talk About** are real because many manufacturers design for regional markets. When I'm designing a film I like to go to stores and create looks for particular characters who would shop there themselves. If you're designing lawyers on location, get those clothes where the story takes place. Lawyers create their own professional armor and you want those suits to reflect their region.

My movies do look like me. **Beetlejuice** (1988) has lots of kooky things that I like and so does **The Witches of Eastwick** (1987). When a designer has actors like Susan Sarandon, Michelle Pfeiffer, and Cher, as I did on that film, they have to have separate and distinct looks. I put Cher in Japanese clothes, Susan in [fashion designer] Betsey Johnson, and neither of their silhouettes had anything to do with Michelle's look as she was in conservative east coast clothing until her character changed. As a designer, it's my job to think about the actors →

ONE FLEW OVER THE CUCKOO'S NEST

(03–04) "There was a company in LA named Arco Sales. A costume designer could call the manager and he would find a garment and send it to you anywhere. Well, I needed some jeans for Jack Nicholson and he sent me two pair, which fit perfectly. I passed the test with Jack and all went forward. Then, I found a hospital in San Francisco that was going out of business and I bought up a lot of scrubs." **(03)** "I wanted a 'Florence Nightingale' coat for Louise Fletcher as Nurse Ratched, and Winnie Brown (costume supervisor) found one for me at Western Costume. She warned me to 'not cut off the hem' if I shortened it and we have been close friends ever since."

I'm going to dress. If I send a shopper out to find the clothes, my show wouldn't look like me. There is a style that makes my work look different from anyone else's. Before **Benny & Joon** (1993), Johnny Depp had already had that Buster Keaton thing going on, but it wasn't full-blown as yet. Pretty much all his clothes came from the old Warner Bros. stage 22's costume stock. It was old junk theoretically, but I'm always sorry that it's not there anymore; they had such great clothes.

The inspiration for my whole career has been used and vintage clothing. Films should not look like television where often the costumes are all ironed neatly. I'm very, very interested in the common man. That started because of **American Graffiti**, dressing just a lot of kids from the valley. The films that I designed where I can remember the actual words in the dialogue are my favorites. The clothes should never get in the way of the writer's words. I don't expect young people who want to become designers to know everything about these complicated matters. We're dealing with costume not just clothes.

On **Return of the Jedi** (1983), George Lucas came to my office every day at five o'clock to talk about the script because there was no written script because of security. We used books ar reference and would look at the photos from the previous **Star Wars** movies. He'd say, "we need 500 of these for a certain scene." I'd call the crew in England and they would pull out the molds and order up some more. I had a wonderful illustrator from the art department who would sit in the office next to mine drawing, which was great because I don't draw. He knew George's style and he would draw all day long, just magnificent. I would go into his office and show him photos of Ancient Japanese warriors and we would adapt them to our characters. We had a big costume shop in San Rafael with 25 stitchers and armor-makers. We all learned so much from working on that film. George and Francis Ford Coppola were my mentors; I owe them each my career!

The Color Purple (1985) was the favorite period film that I have ever designed. We used two different costume houses to manufacture the costumes. Harry Rotz, the milliner at Warner Bros. at the time, made all the hats from my

01 This tiny metal bikini worn by Princess Leia in **Star Wars: Episode VI—Return of the Jedi** helped win Rodgers a Saturn Award

"The clothes should never get in the way of the writer's words."

research photos. All of Danny Glover's hats were made from scratch as his head is larger than any we had in stock.

Sometimes I copied clothes based on research from the Sears, Roebuck catalog. You can't beat Sears, Roebuck for "real" period research. We made all of Oprah's and her sister's clothes right out of the Sears catalog pages, using the entire women's costume workroom at Warner Bros. The men's were made in the tailor shop at Universal. I'd drive back and forth between the two shops. Tommy Velasco, the chief tailor at Universal Studios, taught me so much. Now when I arrive at a tailor shop and the tailor tries to tell me there's something wrong with a sleeve, I'll say, "You have to rotate the sleeve half an inch." They look at me like, "How do you know that?" You can learn so much from a tailor. They have seen it all!

The Schomburg Collection at the New York Public Library had photos of women in juke joints and we used one of them as the source for the red dress that Margaret Avery makes in a scene in **The Color Purple**. I found a version in blue in a costume shop in L.A. and showed it to Steve Spielberg to see if we could do it in red. "Fine," he said, "go ahead." For me, that's better than a drawing. I'd show Steven photos from Sears, Roebuck and say, "This, this, this and this for Oprah" (talking as fast as possible as you only get a few minutes of his time). Working for him is very rewarding and it is fun to see him pleased. I'm really sorry that I never got to work for him again. Eleven of us got nominated for Academy Awards for **The Color Purple**, but none of us won, which I think deeply hurt Steven's feelings.

The director is my hero, that's who I want to be standing by. For Larry [Lawrence] Kasdan, I designed **I Love You to Death** (1990) with Kevin Kline and Tracey Ullman, and **Grand Canyon** (1991) with Kline and Danny Glover. I feel so close to those movies that I can almost recite the scripts. On **Grand Canyon** we had characters from the 'hood, budding gangsters. I took them as a group to one of the big Korean shopping malls that was later burned down during the →

THE FUGITIVE
(02) "'Modern' looks easy, doesn't it? Not so. The producers think it is easy and so they give you very little time. When Harrison Ford was on the run you see him get clothes from a clothing line. We would have shopped at the Goodwill, but we had to have multiples for stunts so it was the army surplus for his costumes and then we broke them down to look old. Of course, when he was dressed to the nines at dinner, the suit was Hart Schaffner Marx as they were a big Chicago firm and I wanted that look."

Los Angeles riots. Larry thought I was crazy to make the trip, but we found incredible stuff there. One of my favorite pieces was a black T-shirt with bullet holes printed across the chest—that's what gangster kids were wearing. As a result of that research, I realized why the gang members never laced up their shoes and let their pants sag. It's a sociological thing; those clothes made it so they couldn't run away, they had no choice but to stand their ground. When designing a film I always feel the worst for the directors, who have a huge job and are trying to say something with the film. Film is art and can be reactive to our political situations. It's so important to have compassion and Larry was courageous about what he was trying to say in **Grand Canyon**.

Another one of my favorite films is **The Hurricane** (1999). When we were shooting the scene where Denzel Washington's character enters the bar, not even the director knew until that moment what the point of view of the film was going to be. If Denzel entered wearing the white dinner jacket, he couldn't have been guilty, because the woman across the street (the witness) would have been able to say in court, "He had on a white dinner jacket." If Denzel entered wearing the black overcoat he could have been guilty. It was very unusual to be standing at the camera in the middle of Newark, New Jersey, waiting to see what the point of view of the film would be based on the color of the costume. We had made up both choices. And

there we were. He put on that white coat, and he went in. He wasn't guilty. That was a trip.

When I designed **Rent** (2005), I didn't have an assistant go pull things for me; I pulled or bought the costumes for the whole show myself. A designer has to think about all the people that they're going to dress. An assistant can't really do it, unless they know your reasoning by heart, and understand why your shows look uniquely like you. There are businesses that buy bales of old clothes, cut them into rags and salvage the buttons, but they keep the good period clothing intact and sort them for easy viewing. There's a place in Iowa that is organized right down to the barrel and the bag. It's a Margaret Mead experience for a designer that I find fascinating. That's why I enjoyed designing **Rent** so much.

Family has been very important in my life and I know so many women and men in costuming who don't have families. When I look at actors and I'm designing their costumes and think about how they are, I believe that I wouldn't have the breadth of knowledge about people if I had not had a long relationship with my husband and the experience of bringing up my children. When you live with children you really see how they dress or how your husband dresses. You can look at all the photos you want, but it works better to know these things by actual experience. Films can look better because of it. **,,**

THE COLOR PURPLE

(02–05) "I sit at my desk and look at the dress that the character Nettie wore in the very last scene. I had found a group of photos at the Schomburg Collection at the New York Public Library that was filled with a mission in Africa from that time period, 1930s, as no one would have been dressed up-to-date at that time out in the bush, and there was a photo of a woman teacher wearing that dress. I copied it. Who could have invented a dress like that? Who would have believed it?" **(02)** "It took me nine hours to fit Whoopi [Goldberg] with her 80 changes. We did it in a day. We never varied with her outfits, as there was no time to find more or switch around. Most of the actors' clothes were set before we left for location. Whoopi was a real champ! All the fittings were great. We all knew that we were working on something so special to our lives. And at this time no one asked me to make a budget up or complained about what we spent." **(04–05)** Illustrations by Haleen Holt.

Ruth Morley

Ruth Morley was a Holocaust survivor who came to America at the age of 14. With limited English language skills, Morley survived school by drawing biology assignments for her classmates in exchange for help with homework. As a teenager with prodigal artistic talent, Morley supported her family by creating greeting cards. Later, she studied painting with the great abstract impressionist Hans Hoffman while posing part-time as an artist's model. When she found a position as a set painter she could no longer continue night school at Cooper Union in New York. Though Morley had focused on painting in the theater, costume designer Rose Bogdonoff became her mentor and champion.

Morley designed costumes for 35 Broadway shows between 1950 and 1988, including **The Miracle Worker** (1959). She found the film adaptation (1962) of the play cathartic, "When I first saw the sunlight shine through the parasol after seeing it on the stage for two years, the real sun with the reflections and shadows of the leaves; the idea of creating films came to me." Morley explained, "I love films, the spontaneity; the challenge. I don't mind being called at midnight and having someone say: 'I forgot to mention, tomorrow at 7 we have 20 extras doing this and 40 extras doing that,' I thrive on it. It's quite different from the theater where it all takes place in one spot. I love going on location." Ruth Morley's brilliantly observed and witty costumes graced 42 memorable films including **Tootsie** (1982). Morley said, "I like working with actors who care more than with actors who say 'Put something on me.' When they care as much as Dustin [Hoffman], I let the actor wear it home."

01 Ruth Morley with Dustin Hoffman on the set of **Tootsie**

02 Kramer vs. Kramer (1979)

03 The Miracle Worker

> "I love films, the spontaneity; the challenge. I don't mind being called at midnight and having someone say: 'I forgot to mention...' I thrive on it."

Her costumes for **Annie Hall** (1977) defined an era, "It's rare for a contemporary film to create a trend. Even the most educated theater people think actors wear their own clothes when the look is modern." Ralph Lauren did not design **Annie Hall**, Ruth Morley did. Journalist Pricilla Tucker interviewed Morley for the *New York Daily News* on April 3, 1978: "Morley started her shopping at Reminiscence, that stay-loose-and-cheap compendium of antique clothes and dyed army surplus. Most of the vests and ties came from thrift shops. The 'period undershirts' and men's hats were bought at Unique Clothing Warehouse. The pleated men's pants, one of the items most copied on Seventh Avenue now, came from the Eaves Costume Co., as did Keaton's men's shoes. The only new pieces were the neckband shirts in menswear shirtings from San Francisco. Morley says she doesn't know where the idea came from that the **Annie Hall** clothes were Ralph Lauren's owned by Diane Keaton. The only piece of Ralph Lauren clothing she wore was 'Alvy'/Woody's jacket which he lent to her on the beach (in the movie). Morley tries to express the personalities of the characters within the context of their environment. Annie Hall was an unformed character, who was not sure which way she was going." With her typical professional modesty Ruth Morley later said, "The whole thing is such a surprise. Like the Sak's ad that says: 'We have the **Annie Hall** jumper.' It's become a household word. I passed the Lord and Taylor windows and almost fainted, they were all **Annie Hall**."

Ruth Morley's other credits include **Taxi Driver**, **Kramer vs. Kramer** and **Ghost**. Sadly Morley passed away in 1991.

04 Taxi Driver (1976)

05 Annie Hall

Penny Rose

"From the beginning perhaps I had the confidence that takes some people much longer to acquire. That confidence blessed me with the ability to just 'attack' projects."

British costume designer Penny Rose started her venerable career working in London's West End theaters. A popular commercial designer, she was introduced early in her career to director Alan Parker, who would become a frequent collaborator, and for whom she designed **Pink Floyd The Wall** (1982). This creative pair continued to work together on three additional films, including the hit musical **Evita** (1996). Starring Madonna as glamorous Argentinian First Lady Eva Perón, the film earned Rose her first BAFTA Award nomination for her elegant costumes.

Rose moved effortlessly between genres, designing the prehistoric fantasy **Quest for Fire** (1981), the quirky comedy **Local Hero** (1983), the authentic period clothes for Richard Attenborough's touching **Shadowlands** (1993) and for Parker's **The Road to Wellville** (1994), both starring Anthony Hopkins. In 1996, she designed her first big-budget action film, **Mission: Impossible** starring Tom Cruise, and by 2010, as a recognized master of the epic, she had designed Mike Newell's **Prince of Persia: The Sands of Time** (2010), a sword-and-sorcery extravaganza based on a video game of the same name, and the action thriller **Unstoppable** (2010), directed by Tony Scott.

Most recently, Rose has been celebrated for her costumes for Disney's **Pirates of the Caribbean: The Curse of the Black Pearl** (2003), **Pirates of the Caribbean: Dead Man's Chest** (2006), **Pirates of the Caribbean: At World's End** (2007), and **Pirates of the Caribbean: On Stranger Tides** (2011). Her design for Johnny Depp's character, Captain Jack Sparrow, has become the iconic prototype for pirate wear, reviving a long-dead genre.

Penny Rose

"My father was very modern and believed in a woman's independence. He always used to say, "If you want something, you should never need to have to ask someone for it. You just work for it and if you can afford it, you make the decision whether you want it or not." That was incredibly inspiring, because my parents did not have expectations just about making a good marriage for me—the expectation was to "make something of yourself." The world was really given to me on a plate; during the summers we traveled to the south of France, winters to Switzerland and on school holidays we'd stay in a hotel in London and spend three nights at the theater. There was no artistic background in my family, except that my parents knew lots of actors.

My parents did not approve of The London Academy of Music and Dramatic Art (LAMDA); we were expected to go to university and get proper English degrees. But academic work gave me considerable difficulty because I'm dyslexic and in the 1950s this was not well understood. That fact eventually persuaded my parents that perhaps the theater might be a practical place for me. So I went to LAMDA where I studied stage management and was taught to sew, and came to really understand actors. Although I was dyslexic I always "got" languages and by 16 I was fluent in three languages.

After three years at LAMDA, I was hired by Fiorucci, the Italian fashion designer, and went to work in Milan. It was the height of swinging London and Fiorucci was emulating that edgy style with an Italian twist. All the women in my family were very smart, but they didn't dress to be noticed, they dressed to be beautifully turned out. If my mother left the house and suddenly realized that she had on navy blue shoes with a black bag, we had to go back inside and swap bags. It was unthinkable that she would venture out with the wrong color purse. I'm not really interested in fashion and was never the kind of person to rush out and buy the latest look, but Fiorucci took me on as an assistant because I spoke fluent Italian and I was the right age, 20ish,

and they thought that I would get the hang of it. It was very lucky.

After returning from Italy, I met a girl at a dinner party who asked if I could give her a hand on a shampoo commercial. Adrian Lyne was the director and afterward he asked me to design a commercial on my own, saying, "Come on, you can do it." Until then, I had never →

01 Madonna as Eva Perón in Alan Parker's musical **Evita**

02 "Every day we dressed between 3,000 and 5,000 people," says Rose of **Evita**

When a look becomes iconic

(03–06) **Pirates of the Caribbean:** "Johnny Depp came to his first fitting already knowing that he wanted to be a rock 'n' roll pirate, only later revealing that the inspiration was Keith Richards (who I subsequently had the honour to dress as Captain Jack's father). Four movies later and Captain Jack has hardly changed his look. It had become so iconic and synonymous with his character that, like Mickey Mouse, it was decided that with the exception of an occasional new vest, weapon or shrunken head, he should always look the same." (06) Illustration by Darrell Warner.

04

03

05

06

01–02 Pink Floyd The Wall

considered working in film. The 1970s' commercial world in London was brimming with incredibly talented people like directors Adrian Lyne, Ridley Scott, Tony Scott and Alan Parker, all of whom gave me a leg up with their blind faith in my ability, and it was a steep learning curve. One day Terence Donovan, a famous stills photographer, said, "I want you to design Marilyn Monroe in the white dress standing over the hot air grid." I did my research, went to the dressmaker, bought the fabric and when the model came in for the fitting I went into a complete panic, wondering, "How do I make the damn thing move?" Not knowing the technical side of film I thought that I was responsible. Determined to make it work, I sewed fishing wire all through the hem of the white dress, then threaded the wire around my hands. By standing at a distance from the model I was able to make the dress move as if it was being blown by the air coming from the grille. When we went to film the commercial, Terence Donovan said to me, "What're you doing? We've got a wind machine!"

Alan Parker was a mentor and probably the biggest influence on my career. He's a wonderful director who does exciting movies that you can really sink your teeth into as a designer, with a massive variety of looks and style. One of Alan Parker's producers had an idea for a prehistoric

movie with apes and asked me to design it. I knew nothing about apes, but he said, "You can do this," and "just study the subject and see what you come up with." I learned how to sew hair onto a lace wig—only it was a lace bodysuit—for **Quest for Fire** (1981). Then I designed **Pink Floyd The Wall** (1982) with Alan Parker and David Puttnam, the successful producer, who was very generous and continued to give me a lot of design work.

In 1984, I became pregnant and decided to stop working for a while, and then I had another baby. At that point, I had designed about eight movies and in my arrogance I thought, "If I ever decide to go back to doing costume design, maybe I'll be okay." Six years later, Alan Parker asked me to design **The Commitments** (1991) and wouldn't take "No" for an answer. **Evita** (1996) followed and then I was introduced to director Richard Attenborough and designed two wonderful movies for him, **Shadowlands** (1993), and **In Love and War** (1996). My career as a costume designer is due to buckets of luck and a lot of determination, considering that I learned costuming while I was doing it. I was never anybody's assistant, and from the beginning perhaps I had the confidence that takes some people much longer to acquire. That confidence blessed me with the ability to just "attack" projects.

> "A costume designer does much more creative work when we've got no money because we have to pull it out of a hat; the challenge is much more exciting."

The great thing about designing any movie is that the job has a beginning, a middle, and an end. Still, it's hard to be a working mother and a working professional at the same time. My girls came on location with me, but most designers are away from home for long periods of time. Location work disrupts our relationships; to anyone hoping to fall in love, get married and have a life, I would say that working in the film business is pretty destructive. My husband and I hung on for 20 years. At 60, I find that the longevity and stress level of a movie is ridiculous. If I lived my life again, I probably would not do the same thing because I missed a lot of my children's growing up.

That being said, as a designer I am surrounded by an incredible group of people, a kind of family in the workplace. Talent alone doesn't make you a good costume designer; it's about your crew. There's a bond. My assistant (and now associate) designer, John Norster,

has been with me for 25 years and I couldn't do it without him; we're a team. Most of the people who work with me in England have been with me for years and I am so grateful for them. They have tremendous commitment to the work, they pay attention if the hat's wrong, or the shoes are too tight, or the makeup artist used a lipstick that doesn't go with the outfit. It's also important to have management skills. If I put a big collar on a costume, I have a long discussion with the hairdresser to make sure it works with the hairstyle. Usually, I'm managing 70 or 80 people in my department and I need to have complete trust in their talent.

When I start designing a big film, I hire a researcher and I spend the first six weeks developing a concept. By this point, I've had several meetings with the director. Obviously, the director is thinking about the story and the characters, and as a designer I work from the director's instruction. For the past six or →

THE ROAD TO WELLVILLE

(03–04) "This delightful script was based on the real story of Dr. Kellogg who set up a health spa in the early 20th century to promote healthy living. Luckily an original manual was found from the original clinic with an invaluable guide to the special clothing and uniforms that people were required to wear. I designed and made everything in London and Rome and rented the formal wear. Bridget Fonda **(03)** had approximately ten changes including swimwear and a wonderful big bloomer cycling costume. We filmed at a historic resort in the Catskills and were a kind of repertory company; the cast and extras played the 250 patients and staff at the clinic. We needed to have on hand all the different costume changes for doctors, porters, patients, waiters, and staff, including bed wear, swimwear, exercise, day clothes, evening wear, and sportswear." **(04)** "John Cusack played the villain and bad boy in **The Road to Wellville**. He had several costumes that were doubled and tripled as his character was always falling into pigpens and other nasty places."

maybe eight years, I've made miniature mannequins dressed as the characters, and poster-size boards for each character and the crowd. This is a comprehensive show-and-tell for meetings with the director, the studio, and the producers. In my experience, directors know immediately what they don't like, and can tell me immediately if my work is headed in the right direction. By the time casting is finished, we are all on the same page.

I've designed quite a lot of armor. Rather than talk about what the armor will look like with the director, it's easier for me to produce a mini version for him, to consider whether the armor is appropriate to the period and right for the film. Obviously, I can't make mini versions of contemporary clothes, which to be honest, I don't like to design. Producers, directors, and actors get sidetracked by fashion, like designer jeans

and Manolo shoes, and they lose sight of the character and how that character should look. More than anything else, textiles give me the most inspiration and buzz. I shop in Los Angeles (where there are great textile stores), in Italy, in France, and I send shoppers to India and Thailand. Sixty-five percent of the time I use the "wrong" side of the textiles for the costume and everything is washed before I cut them— including silks.

Fifty percent of my job is budgeting and

managing a project. A costume designer does much more creative work when we've got no money because we have to pull it out of a hat; the challenge is much more exciting. When I designed **Carrington** (1995) I didn't have any money and actress Emma Thompson was very helpful. "What do you think of the curtains in this room?" I'd ask her. "Shall we make the dress out of those? They seem perfect to me." **Evita** (1996) was my most challenging movie because the action took place from 1930 through 1950 on two continents. Every day we dressed between 3,000 and 5,000 people; Madonna alone had 120 changes. Since I was working on a very tight budget, those clothes (particularly for the crowds) had to work almost more than the actors. Madonna is a huge megastar, but is extraordinarily easy to work with because she knows exactly what she likes and what works for

her. But the low budget, the constant packing and traveling, and the enormity of the background were a stretch for me and for my crew.

Back when I designed **Pink Floyd The Wall**, Alan Parker's producer was Alan Marshall, and his motto was, "It's a cake. Here's your slice, go away and make it work, only come to me if you really have a problem." That was in the days when my team included me and three other people; I didn't have a dye shop, a breakdown shop or a workroom. Nowadays, it's me and a mass of crew on big-budget films with stuntmen and photo doubles, and multiple costumes. The fabric, the trims, the braid, and the buttons are treasures that I have bought and kept, and sometimes I've carried them around with me for ten years. Because the actor's coming in for the fitting tomorrow and working the day after on the film, but luckily I've got just the right thing. →

04 Tom Cruise as Ethan Hunt in **Mission: Impossible**

I think one of my guiding lights is that during the three years at LAMDA I really understood about the actors' process and I get very distressed when I see them being bullied. I don't think people appreciate that they come to work and then spend all day pretending to be somebody else. I marvel at their ability to do that. I go into a fitting room with an actor and if they leave the room looking like the character, then it's a job well done. However difficult they can be, and they can be difficult, I'm very patient because I have a goal. When I get a director who says, "Put her in a black dress," and I think, "Black's not such a great color on her; she's very sallow, she's going to disappear," or whatever the reason, I always stand up for actors because they are the vehicles for the character and for the story. As a designer I try to create a bond between the actors and the director.

My favorite films are the **Pirates of the Caribbean** series (**The Curse of the Black Pearl**, 2003; **Dead Man's Chest**, 2006; **At World's End**, 2007; **On Stranger Tides**, 2011). It's difficult not to be in love with Captain Jack Sparrow—he's a naughty boy, he's funny, and Johnny Depp is such an adorable human being. Before producer

Jerry Bruckheimer gave me the job he asked what "defines" my designs. I said that, "I think I design real clothes." They're dirty, creased, and broken down if it's appropriate. Whether that's my best quality I don't know, but it's what I strive for, whether it is a wedding dress or a

01–02 Clive Owen and Keira Knightley in **King Arthur**

03

ragamuffin's hand-me-downs. I'm honored that Jerry Bruckheimer always asks me back to design **Pirates of the Caribbean**. Rob Marshall directed the last film and he's always worked with Colleen Atwood, so I expected her to be asked, but Jerry and Johnny Depp wanted me to keep the look throughout the series.

Much of the time working with production designers is a duet and I'm always disappointed if they're not interested in what I'm doing, because I'm very interested in what they're doing. I always want our work to blend nicely. On the **Pirates of the Caribbean** movies I've had three different production designers, all extremely talented and quite happy to work as a team. These movies haven't branched out visually or dramatically since the first success, because they are a studio product and everybody likes the product. I've had new characters to develop and design each time, but the essence of each movie hasn't changed.

Original stories and original concepts are rare because the studios want to play it safe. It seems that right now every film is a repeat or the originality of the work is less. I design really big movies all the time and I'm now in my comfort zone. Nobody ever asks me to design a little one although I'd love to try; I'd love to design something set in the 1950s. Whatever it is, I want to stick with movies where I design and make the clothes.

Even if I don't particularly like it, I stick to what my director wants. When we have interference from production people who are not creative I tell them, "Yes, you are the producer, I'm sure your wife has wonderful taste, but I'm working for the director. You have to filter what you need through him." They look at me as if I'm nuts, but I stick to my ground and remain firm. My assumption is that employers hire me for my taste and they should have faith in my ability. I'm dressing human beings playing fictitious characters, and, in some cases, real people being portrayed by actors. So when interference occurs, as it frequently does, I don't shout and scream. If they don't like my taste it's not that I'm doing it wrong, they've got the wrong designer. **"**

03 Jake Gyllenhaal in Mike Newell's epic **Prince of Persia: The Sands of Time**

Julie Weiss

"A designer puts somebody in costume to define who they are, to help them achieve translucency or transparency, unless the script calls for me to hide them. The costume is a canvas that I wrap around the actor and then give it away."

Julie Weiss received her undergraduate degree at the University of California, Berkeley, before earning her MFA at Brandeis University. Her brilliant design for the Broadway production of **The Elephant Man** (1980) earned her both a Tony Award nomination in 1979 and an Emmy Award nomination for the 1982 television adaptation of the play. Impressively, she has received seven Emmy nominations, winning two, the most recent win for **Mrs. Harris** (2005), starring Annette Bening.

From the start, Weiss had incredible opportunities. She designed film legend Bette Davis' last two films, **The Whales of August** (1987) and **Wicked Stepmother** (1989), and for Marlon Brando in **The Freshman** (1990). Weiss received an Academy Award nomination for Terry Gilliam's post-apocalyptic **Twelve Monkeys** (1995). Three years later, she and Gilliam collaborated on Hunter S. Thompson's drug-fueled **Fear and Loathing in Las Vegas** (1998), in which she captured the mania of the original Ralph Steadman illustrations.

Weiss is comfortable working in every genre, evident in her work on Sam Mendes' quiet, modern **American Beauty** (1999); Julie Taymor's **Frida** (2002), a stunning biopic of artist Frida Kahlo (her second Academy Award nomination); the southern anthem, **Steel Magnolias** (1989); and the horror flick **The Ring** (2002). The bejeweled spandex creations Weiss designed for the comedy **Blades of Glory** (2007) provide the film's visual punchline. Weiss recently lent her talents to the period drama **Get Low** (2009) and 1940s' film noir **Shanghai** (2010), also creating Diane Lane's elegant ensembles for **Secretariat** (2010). In 2011, the Costume Designers Guild honored Weiss with a Career Achievement Award.

Julie Weiss

"Costume designers are thieves; before we know what our occupation is, we steal other people's pasts. I'm talking about the deep curiosity of asking why people talk about where they come from or what they should have become, but never who they are in their souls. The answer can be reflected in what they wear, although it has very little to do with costume or garb; it has to do with the right to be who you are, conformist or non-conformist, traditionalist or non-traditionalist. When you begin to see things as a designer, you realize that looking only with your eyes can be both confusing and selfish. There are levels of perception that you might "see" differently, but are not always able to communicate. If you find you're wearing black chiffon to a tennis match, it's not because you don't know how to dress like other people, it's just that you can't bring yourself to do it. I once wore black chiffon to a tennis match—part of me wanting to conform, to wear white, to be part of the audience, to be in the court, but I just couldn't do it without being self-conscious. It would have been easier to conform, but the need to be heard through dress was growing rapidly and the responsibility of being considerate with one's imagination proved confusing.

My mother was a unique individual. She was a writer, poet, and community activist. She was extremely smart and imaginative, and was torn between the longings of independent wanderings and the home address of family. She loved clothes, she loved costumes, but being fashionable and of the moment was very important. Beauty came into being under many definitions, but hopefully "being unique to oneself" would eventually win out and it always did.

My father was a physician at the Veterans Administration Hospital in West Los Angeles when he met my mother. They'd grown up in families where the ticket out was higher education. My grandmother was an extraordinary poker player who loved the game and would give her winnings to charities. In our family you were expected to be responsible for social change. My father's brothers were also physicians and my sister was a great lawyer and judge who started as a public defender defending kids. Working in costume design never occurred to me when I was young; I dreamed of becoming so many different things. My dreams were always changing. I wanted to teach, I wanted to be an anthropologist or a pro bono lawyer practicing out of the back of my car. Whatever it was, I wanted to be part of what was going on in the world. I went on house calls with my father and spent time in his office. He taught me how to look beneath the surface to see the truth about people. Whatever I chose to do, my family was supportive; I was lucky enough to grow up without parameters when it came to questioning anything, but I had to take responsibility for my thoughts. And there was always laughter in our house.

In addition to writing, my mother drew beautifully, but she could never finish her drawings, so I would finish them for her. In second grade my art teacher told us to draw stick figures and I said, "Where's the heart?

01 Sam Raimi's brilliant
A Simple Plan

02–04 Sam Mendes' **American Beauty**. Shown here is Weiss' wonderful sketch and "shopping list" for Carolyn and Jane Burnham, played by Annette Bening and Thora Birch

Where's the flesh? Where is the mind?" I knew that men and women were different, but why weren't the women different from each other? And why couldn't people be different? It was all very confusing.

Before I was ten I went to ballet school and I wasn't very good at it, but I learned about the pose. Looking at myself in the mirror in my leotard or tutu, I knew that wasn't who I was and wondered, "What are the people looking at me seeing?" My family lived in a neighborhood where kids went to parochial schools and public schools. I always noticed the different ways people wore their school clothes and uniforms. After Palisades High I went to college in St. Louis. In my freshman year I was rushing sororities and I was at the beauty shop with my head in the sink,

dressed in Weejun loafers, a Villager blouse, a pleated skirt and a Shetland sweater that itched horribly. I looked down and I said, "Excuse me," and got up, hair still wet, walked out and bought my first dashiki and a pair of sandals. Then my life began to make a little more sense.

The next year I transferred to UC Berkeley where your responsibility was to tell the truth about what you knew. As a liberal arts major I could study anything I wanted; the arts and sciences were equally accessible, and it was easy to do well there because it was such an exciting time, Martin Luther King spoke and Janis Joplin sang. Painting classes were a bit of a problem because I had trouble staying on the canvas; I'd go off the canvas and down the street. I took a few theater classes, worked on Harold →

> **"When you begin to see things as a designer, you realize that looking only with your eyes can be confusing and there are levels of perception that you might 'see' differently."**

Pinter's **The Caretaker** and painted an elaborate backdrop for a love scene in **The Revenger's Tragedy** with my initials hidden everywhere. The director wasn't too pleased when he noticed this on opening night. In my senior year, three professors—Henry May, who had been a set designer for GE Theater, Travis Bogard, the great authority on Eugene O'Neill, and William Oliver, who was part of the Theatre of the Absurd—called me in and asked what I planned to do after graduation. I told them I wasn't sure yet, I just knew that I wanted to make a difference. "We've been thinking about you," they said. "There's a program in theater at Brandeis we feel could offer you a world of challenges. Especially when we're living in a time when political voices need to be heard." What better place than the theater. "I guess I have to apply?" I asked. "No," they answered, "there's a space being held for you if you want it." And I started to cry. "Why do you care?" I said. "We believe you have something to say," they told me.

So I went to Brandeis and that was where I learned how lucky I was to have grown up with a level of visual wealth that all the time I'd thought I had been missing. But I needed discipline, that you can't be afraid to try out your own thoughts in front of the world, and not hide when the opinions come in. I learned that compromise was a good thing, that in the theater you can't work alone and you don't want to. As a costume designer I must see what is in front of me; I have to take myself out of it, to see the clarity of the word, to find out how the director sees the script, and who the actor wants to be. I take the role, find out where that truth is and only then do I bring myself back in. In a sense I'm dressing the space between the words, taking a character and enhancing them, so that when it gets to the stage (or later the screen) the character belongs to everyone. A designer puts somebody in costume to help define who they are, to help them achieve translucency or transparency, unless the script calls for me to hide them. The costume is a canvas that I wrap around the actor and then give it away. I'm still learning about the right time to give it away.

After Brandeis, I moved to New York to become a designer. I heard that the union exam was really hard and that they only took a few people, but the assignment was Pirandello's **Henry IV**, where madness is confronted, which I thought I could manage. So I took the exam and to my shock I got in the union. I had to draw costume sketches in front of a jury. I was petrified because I always needed help drawing hands and feet. I still need help, which is why the costume designs in my sketches have so many pockets.

Now that I had graduated and I was in the union, I needed to learn from people who had lived their education. My goal was to work with Ray Diffen at his costume shop, but I didn't get the job. Three days later he called saying I had it. "Did you like my portfolio?" I asked. In my mind I can hear Ray Diffen saying: "Don't be a fool, darling. You left your yellow notebook here, and I got four stars—the highest rating you gave any costume house." He put me to work gluing jewelry. At that point he was working on **Jesus**

01   Diane Lane in **Secretariat**

02   Adrien Brody in **Hollywoodland**

03   Julia Roberts in **Steel Magnolias**

Christ Superstar (1971). One Friday he asked if I knew how to macramé and I told him "Of course," but I had to spend the weekend learning how because I had exaggerated my skill. That Monday I came to work with four small samples, which had taken me an entire weekend to figure out. "What are you doing here?" he said, "I let you go." "I didn't know," I said, never having been fired. Then he said, "What are those?" And I showed him the samples. "Fine, darling," he said, "make 40 square feet of that for the Chrysalis scene." And I cried.

While I was at Diffen's I was offered my first Broadway show with Howard Bay, the Chairman of the Theater Design program at Brandeis, who was also an accomplished set designer, having designed **Man of La Mancha** on Broadway. Being my first Broadway show in a contemporary setting I had a hard time finding the clothes; I wanted to design them, I wanted to have them made, but I couldn't afford it. After trying everywhere I finally went to Ray Diffen and to the best of my memory, he said with great authority: "It took you long enough." "You knew I had this job?" I said. "Who do you think recommended you?" When I told him I had no money, he said he would do it for almost nothing. "Am I that good?" I asked, astonished. "Absolutely not, but if I don't do this for the price of the fabric, you will go to another shop and blame your costume problems on them. If you work with me, you'll know how much more you have to learn as a designer." And there was to be no blame allowed.

I got a recommendation to meet Dorothy Jeakins who was designing **The Duchess of Malfi** at the Mark Taper Forum. I met with her and she hired me to assist her. She also had Joe Tomkins as another assistant. He got to do all the fittings and help her pick the buttons. She was great on buttons. All Dorothy Jeakins' assistants wanted to be part of two things; her extraordinary swatch book with a description of each character, and the buttons. The buttons. The buttons. The buttons…The buttons could hold the history, what somebody touched to get in and out of their soul. "And you, Julia," she said—she called me Julia, →

BOBBY

(04) "Instead of a wedding gown this dress would have been something that she [Lindsay Lohan] would have bought for her prom. 'The Prom' is a big moment in a teenager's life and in an adult's photo memory. It was what she had in her closet. Hopefully, this pastel plaid organza dress would show how young the character was and how this was not the wedding that she was supposed to have had."

04

FRIDA

(01–03) "People get dressed for many reasons, to disguise themselves, to copy other people, to show their social stature and to draw attention to themselves. The key to costume design is to get past the clothes. The clothes should not fight what the camera is capable of catching—that little moment, that glimpse into a person and who they really are. In **Frida**, I was answerable to an existing story. I couldn't possibly compete with how Frida Kahlo dressed. When she walked down the street, she exuded an aura. She didn't demand, 'Look at me,' rather, she said, 'This is who I am,' and that is the major difference." **(02–03)** Weiss' sketches for Diego Rivera and Frida Kahlo.

04–05 Robert Duvall and Bill Murray in **Get Low**

06 Benicio Del Toro and Johnny Depp in **Fear and Loathing in Las Vegas**

"shall take Goya's *Los Caprichos* and *Disasters of War* and do those who have gone mad and been hurt by war." Dorothy's clothes let people be alive inside them; the costume she designed became the same as skin. From Dorothy I learned that when you assist somebody you help in any way you can, so that when they come into work they can begin with what's in front of them, an extraordinary lesson for me. I loved her sketches; the paper breathed. They were so different to my crooked way of thinking.

A teaching job came up in the drama department at Stanford University that I was probably too young for, but I needed to solidify my lessons in literature. What have we learned in war? What happens when you're betrayed? What is bliss? While I was there I designed for the San Francisco Opera and for school opera productions and plays. Then I had an opportunity to work at the Mark Taper Forum in Los Angeles under the direction of Gordon Davidson, and later I returned to New York to design a soap opera, primarily because they had the best cameras and I wanted experience working with that equipment. And anyway my parents were happy because they thought they knew where I was between the hours of one and two in the afternoon when the soap opera aired. I worked →

in the theater in the evening. One of the soap directors was Jack Hofsiss, who hired me to design **The Elephant Man** (1980). I was lucky enough to be nominated for a Tony Award in 1979 and in 1982 for an Emmy for the television adaptation. When my designs for the **The Dollmaker** (1984) won the Emmy I was proud, because it wasn't about traditional beauty and because although it was a period piece, I'd learned that my job was to show the audience people who looked like somebody they knew. In this business there are designers that I admire who know how to do the glamour. I've been trained to do that too, but something happens to me when a person merges with who they are and what they want to be: and then everything gets rained on. That's when I know I can help, no matter what the year or period is. I also received an Emmy for **A Woman of Independent Means** (1995) in which Sally Field plays a woman over seven decades. When I was lucky enough to be nominated for Academy Awards, it was for **Twelve Monkeys** (1995) and **Frida** (2002), movies about non-traditional characters who had their own take on time and reality.

In my career I've been fortunate to work with legends—Angela Lansbury, Maureen Stapleton, Geraldine Fitzgerald, Geraldine Page, Henry Fonda, Robert Duvall, and Gregory Peck among others. They all took time to sit me down and say, "Okay, take a look at this, then look again, and look again." Marlon Brando took extra time when I worked with him on **The Freshman** (1990). In the scene with Matthew Broderick where he was saying goodbye, Brando asked the director if he was satisfied and Andy Bergman said, "Absolutely." "Can I try it without words?" Brando suggested, and I watched and began to understand the leanness of the cacophony of all those sounds, the colors, and the clothes. Although Brando was at his largest then, he abounded with sexuality, he owned the room and I truly believed that I was designing for one of the most handsome and alluring men alive. When I worked on the film **Get Low** (2009) with Robert Duvall, his character spoke at his own funeral. We all ran to the set, because we knew he

How inspiration happens

(01) "I was in the gynecologist office and the doctor was wearing two pairs of rubber gloves. I said, 'Excuse me, but when you are delivering a baby, is it true that the first thing a newborn child feels is the slap of a rubber glove? Is there no more the comfort of the human hand as the first entry touch?' The doctor responded, 'I'm afraid so.' I got on my cell phone and immediately reached our costume department on **Twelve Monkeys** and said, 'Seal everything! Take away touch! Wrap everything in plastic! Our future is here!' Although I love the pageantry of design, that's not always how the inspiration happens. This time it wasn't about silk and jewels. I respect traditional beauty, but something happens to me when I design a beautiful gown. I desire mud stains on its train, sweat stains from the tryst, and love letters stuffed in the cleavage."

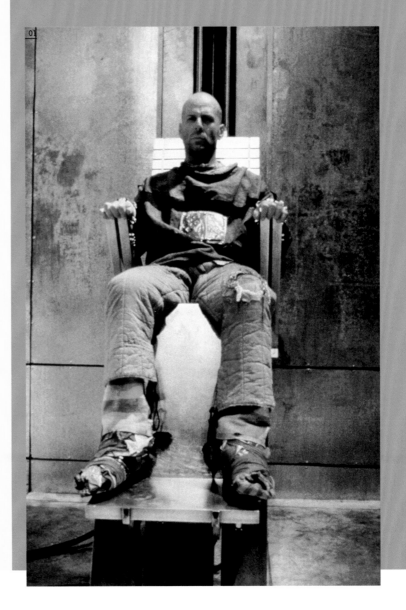

BLADES OF GLORY

(02) "I found the world of ice skating to be full of visual excitement; there were traditions and new concepts. There were costumes for those who skated in pairs, costumes for solos, costumes in which one could do triple axles, and costumes that would not injure the skater if they fell. **Blades of Glory** had a strong visual concept. Any actor who would dress like a peacock complete with tail feathers and strut around with such aplomb that people wanted to try the outfit on would make any costume designer grateful. Any actor who would get excited and feel secure putting on a one-piece stretch jumpsuit with red and orange Swarovski crystal flames and with a back so low that one could use the great word 'risqué' meant that I had landed in heaven."

could possibly be filmed in one take and at that moment the empty hanger didn't matter, because these are the kind of moments that make us rich.

Bette Davis helped me a great deal. She guided me and was both tough and supportive, beginning when I worked with her on the mini series **Little Gloria. . .Happy at Last** (1982). We were in the fitting room at Western Costume and I asked if she was going to have her own dresser. She looked at me aghast. "Don't you know who I am?" she said. "Don't you know what I've done? You're a fool. You're an idiot." She was speaking quite loudly, gesturing with her cigarette, in that magnificent voice I'd heard in the movies and all I could think was, "Bette Davis is yelling at me just like in **All About Eve**." As she got up to leave I managed to say, "Ms. Davis, will you please stay? I need you for a minute. I need you to help me." "Fine," she said, "What is it?" And I said, "I'm very sorry I said that. I am still naïve in these areas. But I do know I'm going to be in this business a long time and I want to do well, and I need your help. So if you like the costume then please help me." I don't know how I conjured up the courage to speak to Ms. Davis like that, but somehow I did and it changed everything for me. I subsequently designed her costumes for **The Whales of August** (1987) and in her later

years she'd call me if she wanted something unusual, all the while sharing her luscious stories.

In my career I've designed for theater, television, and films. I just want to tell stories. When I started in costume design I fought unnecessarily; I wanted to do more. But I learned that costume designing is more than fulfilling for me. I'm allowed to be a filmmaker. I know that film is a business, I understand the commercial end of making a movie, but I also understand the excitement of working on a magnificent production. There will always be people who have doubts that dreams can come to screens, but there will never be any doubt that the word "action" will definitely be heard. I used to fear post-production, where in the editing room I always thought my best costumes were cut, but now I want to be a part of post-production; I want to be part of the digital age. I want to be able to see that way, but I also want that screen to sweat and to cry and to moan—to be human. The future is a combination of the two and I want to be on that bridge. And I always hope my level of curiosity exceeds my ego; I don't want to be hired for what I've already done. Bette Davis said, "Fasten your seatbelts," but I want to unhook mine. 〞

Janty Yates

"With film design you have to climb into
the story and allow it to absorb into your bones.
To be authentic, the designer has to run the
timeline and the character arc. You have to live
and experience each character's history."

Born in Hertfordshire, England, designer Janty Yates attended a private pattern-cutting college before she made her foray into feature films in 1981 as Penny Rose's assistant on Jean-Jacques Annaud's **Quest for Fire** (1981). Her first feature design credit came a decade later on **Bad Behavior** (1993), which was followed by the romantic comedy **The Englishman Who Went Up a Hill But Came Down a Mountain** (1995); **Jude** (1996), starring Kate Winslet; and **Plunkett & Macleane** (1999), directed by Jake Scott, son of acclaimed director Ridley Scott.

Impressed with her work on **Plunkett & Macleane**, Ridley hired Yates to design his Roman epic, **Gladiator** (2000). She was rewarded with an Academy Award and a BAFTA Award nomination, and Scott has kept her very close ever since as one of his key artistic collaborators. Her relationship with Scott has spanned genres and periods: from the 12th-century crusades in **Kingdom of Heaven** (2005), to the wide lapels of 1970s' New York City in **American Gangster** (2007), to the year 2080 for **Prometheus** (2012), a prequel to **Alien** (1979). Yates has also designed legions of characters that can be seen in the 25,000 costumes in Scott's **Robin Hood** (2010).

In addition to her busy schedule with Ridley Scott, Yates has found time to design the World War II drama, **Charlotte Gray** (2001), with Cate Blanchett; and Annaud's gritty Stalingrad siege picture **Enemy at the Gates** (2001), starring Jude Law and Joseph Fiennes. Her glamorous "Old Hollywood" look for **De-Lovely** (2004), the musical biopic about composer Cole Porter, was sublime.

Janty Yates

"When I was a teenager in London, there was a British fashion magazine called *Nova* that I was mad about. It described itself as "The new kind of magazine for a new kind of woman." I've still got about ten of them. If you recall the swinging 1960s—Mary Quant, Barbara Hulanicki from Biba—the fashion of that period was so exciting; I lived and breathed it. My mother was a bastion of country living, all tweeds and hats, and she put me in these terrible party dresses that had frills and bows. She dressed me as a child and I didn't want to be a child; it was mortifying. Some of my interest in fashion was a rebellion against my mother's taste in clothes. I must have made 20 or 30 miniskirts a season for me and my friends. My time wasn't completely spent in my studio wildly sewing, though; I rode my horse and went to gymkhanas. I also went to the movies constantly in those days; we had a local cinema—one theater, not the multiplexes that abound today. Film had a huge influence on me and I remember going to see **Lawrence of Arabia** (1962) about three or four times, just for the beauty of it.

During my late teens I attended Katinka School of Dress Designing in South Kensington, London, where I studied design, dressmaking, and pattern cutting. Then I worked in a wholesale fashion house in the East End and for *Vogue* and Butterick Patterns in my twenties. I then did a huge amount of work in commercials, first as an assistant's assistant and then as an assistant, and then designing commercials on my own. On two or three films I served as a costume assistant standby with Pip Newbery. As these things often happen, she recommended me to design a short film when her life became too stressful to take the job. Designing two or three short films inspired me and gave me confidence to do more. Pip introduced me to Penny Rose, who hired me on **Quest for Fire** (1981), because she was allergic to fur. My job was mostly cutting up bearskins—which, of course, you can't do these days. **Quest for Fire** was my first movie on location.

When I begin a new job I'm like a dog with a bone, unable to think of anything else. I buy books by the millions and go to libraries and museums endlessly, and this research goes on until halfway through the production. Everything is about filling as many research files or folders as possible. And often I give my research folders to the hair and makeup department. Of course, now you can get quite a bit of information on the web, but to really get the feel of it you need to hold stuff, to actually see the garment, to feel the fabric and to physically have the helmet in your hand. For **Gladiator** (2000), when I was in Rome all I had to do was walk round and stare at the statues. Everything I needed was on Trajan's Column, which is covered with a relief of thousands of military uniforms with armies marching left, right and center.

The first briefing with the director is what actually kickstarts my research; Ridley Scott is great for art references. On **Gladiator**, he suggested, "Look at Alma-Tadema for the crowd." Sir Lawrence Alma-Tadema painted Roman scenes in the late 1800s and early 1900s, using pastels—I used pistachios, pinks, almonds and sky blue for the extras. For the principals, Ridley mentioned Georges de La Tour, a French artist of the Renaissance who used sumptuously rich colors with tiny gilded details in his costumes. "Gnarly" was a favorite expression of Ridley's, applicable to all fabrics/armors/leather. He wanted it very textured and aged. For **Robin Hood** (2010), Ridley was inspired by Bruegel and this gave me a sweeping feel for the look of the film. Artists are a great inspiration; when I leave my art books I am full to bursting with energy and just want to start designing. This is a research process that I now know inside out.

After research, sketching is absolutely essential. I employ an illustrator on the costume design team who stays with me so that I can work with them on a day-to-day basis. Lora Revitt has illustrated for me for the last five or six years. We work closely for weeks in pre-production, during shooting and whenever something comes up in the script that needs illustrating.

At the beginning of a film I try to get a meeting with the director of photography, the production

> **"Artists are a great inspiration; when I leave my art books I am full to bursting with energy and just want to start designing."**

designer and the director, so that we can chart our color palette and so that everyone is on the same road. We work very collaboratively; no one wants to have a beige wall with a beige suit in front of it or to lose the actress in a green dress in a green room.

Casting on any film is hugely important. If the director gives me at least a semblance of an idea of whom he and the casting agent are thinking of for any role, then I can form a three-dimensional image of the character, keeping that particular actor in mind. Casting may not necessarily be confirmed and the idea for a part is sometimes completely thrown out the window at the last minute. This happens often in this era of late casting. By the same token, a good actor can inhabit a costume that wasn't designed especially for them.

I designed a few films for Michael Winterbottom in the 1990s. Michael is a wonderful, exciting, and challenging director. His vision is very pared down, linear and gritty. On **Jude** (1996) he wanted simplicity and

authenticity, no frills or furbelows, which was hard, as the period, especially for women, was quite ornate. It came down to sourcing original garments and also good breakdown and aging. **Welcome to Sarajevo** (1997) was a huge challenge as we filmed in Sarajevo only six months after the Dayton Agreement. On my preliminary recce, I was sitting in the street where a bomb had exploded only months before, and I was so impressed at the strength and spirit of the people there. Men wore suits, women were well turned out, their hair was done and they were wearing makeup. It was as if their spirit refused to be quelled by the violence. While shooting all over on location it was stressed that we must avoid all the grassy areas due to the unexploded mines everywhere.

One of the compliments a designer can receive is, "I didn't notice the costumes." When I've designed the most extraordinarily beautiful things for a royal family or the court, I'd hate it if those costumes aren't noticed, but in a contemporary cinema or television drama, you →

01 Michael Winterbottom's starkly realistic **Jude**

01

> "When I begin a new job I'm like a dog with a bone, unable to think of anything else. I buy books by the millions and go to libraries and museums endlessly."

don't want the costume to be doing the acting. With film design you have to climb into the story and allow it to absorb into your bones. To be authentic, the designer has to run the timeline and the character arc. You have to live and experience each character's history.

Ultimately the designer usually adapts to each director's vision. Of course, there are a huge number of conversations with the director, because even though you've got the sweeping brief of the story, there are always important design details. I've been amazingly lucky to work with Ridley Scott several times; he is one of the most visual and painterly directors in the world. Ridley graduated from the Royal College of Art and started life as a production designer, so his visual appreciation is always stimulating and inspiring. Now, Ridley paints with light in the cinema.

Jean-Jacques Annaud's vision of World War II on **Enemy at the Gates** (2001) was completely different to Gillian Armstrong's on **Charlotte Gray** (2001), which was set in the same time period. **Enemy at the Gates** was about the siege of Stalingrad and Jacques Annaud wanted everyone to be completely, utterly filthy and degraded, and their costumes distressed to the point of rags. They were in siege mode and consequently lived in their uniforms for up to five years and didn't have the opportunity to ever get clean. Gillian Armstrong's vision for **Charlotte Gray**, about the German Army's occupation of France, portrayed the soldiers as a pristine, perfectly turned out invading force; marching along, the army looked like an immaculate gray cube.

Looking back at my career thus far, I've designed costumes for 180 AD, the 12th century, 1860, the 1940s, 1970, and contemporary. I love every film that I've worked on for different reasons, yet I don't know what the definable element of my design style would be. **Gladiator** was probably the most challenging film, because I had never been involved in designing a film containing so many armies, so much armor and

so many battles before. I was lucky I had a fantastic supervisor, a fantastic assistant designer, and an amazing team. We dressed 3,500 extras every day for at least three months. When we were shooting at the Coliseum in Malta, we were getting up at 2.30 a.m. to fit and dress them for the day. It was terrifying! Certainly I never dreamt I'd be nominated for an Oscar for **Gladiator**, let alone actually win one.

If forced to choose, I might say **Kingdom of Heaven** (2005) was my favorite film that I designed, and I was working with Ridley again. When I opened the script there were 5,000 Saracens and 1,000 Christians. We traveled throughout Spain, which was very hard, and then we went all around Morocco. But I had a great team—including a great military specialty team, which I never had before. To work with my own team all the time would be ideal, but it's a matter of their availability. There are two or three supervisors I've tried to keep, but there's no guarantee given the timing of productions.

Getting along with people is essential. But the one indispensable quality a costume designer

01 Jude Law in **Enemy at the Gates**

must have is a good eye; I really believe that's the most important talent. With the "eye" the designer gets the feel of the characters, with the feel you get the concept of the director, and with the concept you get the atmosphere of the story. It doesn't have to come through formal training; it's intuitive, it's just there, a natural thing. Actors perform well if they love the feel of their clothes, and if the designer makes the fittings special and everyone gets along.

The last film I designed in 2011 was **Prometheus**, which is set in 2080, again for Ridley. It's the prequel to **Alien** (1979) and we're shooting at Pinewood Studios. **Prometheus** is a huge video-effects-based film and has a massive amount of green screen. I've approached the costume design by process of elimination. It's gone from puffy NASA suits down to skinny body-hugging space suits with armor. We were having practical problems with the design of the helme, as Ridley said that during **Alien** the original was just a regular helmet and the actors would get claustrophobic unless their helmets had air holes.

More recent films like **The Fifth Element** (1997, costumes designed by Jean-Paul Gaultier) had a fan blowing air in the helmets, but we have gone so far beyond that now. But now we have created something of utter beauty. The helmets in **Prometheus** have nine working screens, four around the neck and five in the actual helmet, air pumping through them, LED lighting throughout, are wired for sound, and have cameras, all of which the costume department has been responsible for right down to the last tiny little wire. My team had to become special effects artists; without our work, VFX would have had to project the nine screens in post-production for every actor, and both the lighting and air would have had to be special effects.

My special-effects costume-prop maker, Ivo Coveney and his team, and one of my assistant designers, Michael Mooney, who's marvelous with minute detail, constructed the futuristic armor. The two of them got together with my first-assistant costume designer, Andrea →

CHARLOTTE GRAY

(02) "This period is a feast for the eyes and Cate Blanchett (Charlotte Gray) wore everything with her consummate elegance. Nearly every garment in the film was original and the garments that I designed were built in original fabrics. I had the knits handmade in original wools, and even had complicated pattern repeat skirts woven in the North of England. The accessories were originals and the new gloves that I designed were hand stitched. This jacket was a soft, but strong wool in plum and the simple rust wool chapeau was color coded to keep Charlotte's sojourn in France in a woodland palette. Her time in London was a more urban and bolder color palette of monochromes with a dash of color."

GLADIATOR

(01–03) "Russell Crowe had ten different sets of
armor throughout the film to show the passage of time.
Every set had eight repeats (copies) and each set had
around 20 components. Maximus (Russell Crowe)
loved this cuirass and with each win he would fund a
new sculpted embellishment in silver on the front. For
the same reason, by the time he fought the emperor
Commodus (Joaquin Phoenix), he wore more armor,
and his greaves, manica, and shoulder lorica were more
detailed. All of the tunics in the film were kept long
because I wanted the very masculine look reminiscent
of the Scottish kilt. Every garment, either fabric or leather,
was painstakingly hand-sewn. During the film I employed
five entirely different teams of special-effects costume-
prop armor specialists."

ROBIN HOOD

(01–02) "King John (Oscar Isaacs) inherited his helmet from his brother King Richard. It is an exact replica from the statue of Richard the Lionheart outside the Houses of Parliament in London. Weta Studios in New Zealand made King John's golden chainmail. All the embroidery of the crest and the surcoat trim were gold bullion woven in India. This costume may be the only one in the film that was not aged, because King John had no action whatsoever and was extremely vain. Historically, John constantly wore many gold bangles, rings on every finger, earrings and jeweled pendants. This was fun to recreate, but sadly none of these are visible in this photo." **(02)** Illustration by Lora Revitt detailing King John's "Palace wear."

Cripps, and made all my armor, using car bumper rubber and things like that. Another costume prop company, FBFX SFX, made all the Emperor's armor in **Gladiator**, and Robert Allsopp made all of Russell Crowe's armor. These days, costume props are becoming a huge business. They're our unsung heroes of the costume design department. On **Prometheus**, I started with the premise that every costume had to function on a real human body. I went from there, developing the design and allowing it to evolve, and my crew managed to have it all ready in four months. **Prometheus** has been a learning curve, but fun and really exciting. I am so proud of what my costume department has accomplished. "

03 Russell Crowe in Ridley Scott's
American Gangster

Creating realistic chainmail

(04–06) "We made the chainmail breakthrough on **Kingdom of Heaven**. Film chainmail had always been knitted in cotton and sprayed silver. Real steel chainmail was impossible to wear due to inordinate weight and aluminum chainmail is also weighty and uncomfortable. The Weta workshop in New Zealand started making lightweight chainmail, painstakingly, with two men, by hand, on **Lord of the Rings**. When we got in touch with them they were in the process of setting up a 2000-strong factory in China. Thanks to them, we were able to costume all actors plus stunts, in lightweight realistic chainmail made in 'hips and pc' (the car-bumper-strength type plastic that the chainmail is made from). Each actor's helmet was custom-built, per character, the fit is so important in bcu (big close-up). The most beautiful helmets were the intricately engraved Saracen helmets, uniforms and armor that were designed in collaboration with my associate military designer David Crossman." **(06)** Illustration by Lora Revitt for Richard the Lionheart, played by Iain Glen in the film.

Mary Zophres

"A designer has to be able to engage and I love the collaboration of it all. It's also very important to love actors and to love the process of turning them into their characters and I do."

Growing up in Fort Lauderdale, Florida, Mary Zophres worked in her family's clothing store where her design talent was immediately recognized. While attending Vassar College as an art major she fell in love with the movies. After graduating, Zophres stayed in New York and found her way as a costume PA on Oliver Stone's **Born on the Fourth of July** (1989) for designer Judy Ruskin. She worked as an assistant costume designer for Ruskin on three more films, including the comic hit **City Slickers** (1991).

Confident that costume design was her destiny, Zophres left New York for Los Angeles. Determined to assist designer Richard Hornung, she worked with him on three films, including Joel and Ethan Coen's **The Hudsucker Proxy** (1994). When Hornung became too ill to design **Fargo** (1996), Zophres stepped in and a close creative partnership with the Coens was launched. Zophres has designed ten films for the Coens, including **The Big Lebowski** (1998), the 1930s' allegorical adventure, **O Brother, Where Art Thou?** (2000), and **No Country for Old Men** (2007). Their most recent lyrical collaboration, the western remake **True Grit** (2010), earned Zophres her first Academy Award nomination.

Zophres has managed to design and master a wide variety of films in between Coen projects, including the Farrelly brothers' comedy hits **Dumb and Dumber** (1994) and **There's Something About Mary** (1998), Jon Favreau's **Iron Man 2** (2010), and **Cowboys & Aliens** (2011). Some of her major credits include Oliver Stone's **Any Given Sunday** (1999), the critics' darling **Ghost World** (2001), and Steven Spielberg's playful period piece **Catch Me If You Can** (2002).

Mary Zophres

" When I was seven, Dad opened his own clothes store called "The Bottom Half," a unisex boutique. My parents met in California where my mother was a schoolteacher and my father was a structural engineer. They moved back to Fort Lauderdale, Florida, to join my extended family of Greek immigrants. Growing up in a clothing store really affected me, although I didn't realize it until much later in my life. After school, I did my homework at the store; then I'd fold clothes and occasionally work behind the register. My mother tells people, "Mary's been dressing people since she was seven years old," because I could instantly size a customer and easily guess their waist and inseam, and I was good at suggesting clothing choices that worked for them.

My high-school essay, "What it means to me to be Greek," won a bonanza of scholarship money for college and I decided to head north. My time at Vassar turned out to be a life-changing experience. As a studio art and art history major, I planned to work in museums until my junior year when I took my first film class. Our first screening was François Truffaut's **Day for Night** (1973), a movie about making a movie, and I'll never forget it. It hadn't occurred to me that you could work on a movie, and from that moment on, I took tons of filmmaking classes. One week I would be in a movie, the next week I would be lighting or shooting a movie, or designing the sets and the costumes; I got some

experience of what it takes to make a film. When I told my mother that I thought I could be a production designer, a costume designer or a cinematographer, she asked immediately, "Why not a director?" My parents instilled in me a belief that I could do anything that I wanted to do. At the same time, they told me, "'The Bottom Half' is yours, if you want it."

My move to New York City after graduation was a huge shock to my parents. For the first six months, I worked as a waitress and as a bartender because I had no money to work for free, as was the rule then, as a production assistant on a film. One day, as I walked from my waitressing job to my bartending job, I passed the Norma Kamali store on 56th Street. In the window, they showed an incredible fashion video that she directed. I went inside and asked, "Do you guys need help?" Incredibly, they did, and I worked there for six months on Kamali's visual displays and videos, while continuing to tend bar. Between all my jobs, I was literally putting money in a sock in my drawer, I saved enough so that I could afford to work (for free) as a PA on a movie.

My friend Robert Grindrod got me a job as a PA for costume designer Judy Ruskin on **Born on the Fourth of July** (1989). When I arrived, Judy was busily prepping in a loft space. There was a big pile of clothes in the center of the room. She said, "These are going to the dry cleaners, but we want to sort them into time periods. Can you divide this into the 1950s, 1960s and 1970s?" As

A SERIOUS MAN

(01) "Larry (Michael Stuhlbarg) was so vividly captured in the script that this is exactly how I imagined him looking when I read it. When he is not teaching, I wanted Larry in short-sleeve plaid shirts, flat front pants and glasses. Even though the film took place in 1968, his look and the look of the movie is more conservative than you would associate with the era of Jefferson Airplane, since the story was set in a conservative Jewish suburb in the American Midwest."

01

a thrift-store junkie I'd always dressed in vintage mixed with stuff from my parents' store. Without knowing it, I had developed a working knowledge of 20th-century clothing. I found myself standing in her loft, writing up the dry cleaning tags like a little robot, thinking, "This is fun, I'm comfortable doing this, this is where I belong." It was such a definitive moment; I just knew, "This is totally going to work out for me, I'm going to be a costume designer." I'll never forget it. Judy invited me to work on location in Texas and put me in charge of dressing all the extras. Although I had never worked on a movie, I was totally comfortable and good at it. After that I never looked back.

When I returned to New York, I knew that I needed more schooling in costume design. Every designer needs to know the construction of a garment to communicate with their cutter/fitter about how they want their clothes to look. I had no idea how to cut a garment or how to make a hat, and to boost my confidence I took classes at the Fashion Institute of Technology in pattern-making, millinery, and textile manipulation. Having confidence is extremely helpful in the film business—this sense of security helps tremendously in dealing with the rejection and weirdness in the politics of movies.

I was in college when I saw **Raising Arizona** (1987) and I remember thinking "Oh my God, that movie's great!" Then, when Judy Ruskin and I were in Santa Fe, New Mexico, working on **Young Guns II** (1990), we decided to drive an hour to Albuquerque to see a screening of **Miller's Crossing** (1990). I was developing this thing for the Coens' movies. The late Richard →

02–03 Zophres' mood board of ideas for the film **Sirens** and how this was translated in the film itself

Hornung was Joel and Ethan Coen's longtime costume designer—I had loved Richard's work since **Raising Arizona** and I had always wanted to work with him. After Judy and I returned to New York, I decided that the city is great, but not without money; I was itching to move to Los Angeles. When Judy's friend, costume designer Ellen Mirojnick, moved to Los Angeles to design **Radio Flyer** (1992), she took me with her as her assistant. Although that version of **Radio Flyer** was cancelled, Ellen and I have been friends ever since.

That same year, Richard Hornung was designing **Barton Fink** (1991), and when I became free again I offered to be his PA. At the time, Mark Bridges was Richard's longtime assistant designer. My duties as PA meant that I never laid eyes on Joel and Ethan, but I didn't care, because I saw Richard's clothes in the warehouse. Mark and Richard would have costume fittings and I'd size the clothes and then put them back in stock. When I assisted Richard on **This Boy's Life** (1993) we hit it off. And when we finished shooting I was ready to apply to graduate school. Richard said, "Work with me instead. It'll be exactly like grad school, but you'll get paid." And he was right. Richard Hornung was my graduate school just as Judy Ruskin had been my undergraduate school. As their assistant, I was constantly trying to help them

realize their vision. There's not a day that goes by that I don't think of them, something that they taught me, or that we laughed about.

Richard captured every character he designed. There was always a touch of whimsy present, but his designs were never over the top. A tight color palette and the use of a consistent silhouette were hugely important to him and he knew how to capture a certain period for the background extras. He taught me how to age and dye, and nothing went directly from a fitting to the screen without being dyed. That was intuitive for him and it became intuitive for me. That's the reason why my movies look the way they do.

Before I worked as an assistant designer on **The Hudsucker Proxy** (1994) someone asked, "Are you ready to design?" and I answered, "I wouldn't know where to start." **The Hudsucker Proxy** was such a big movie on such a grand scale, and had a lot of background and tons of principals. Faced with so much responsibility, I realized that I knew how it should look, that I didn't have to go to Richard for advice. It was exactly what had happened that day I was sorting the laundry at Judy's and I suddenly felt, "I can do it."

My theory is, the minute that you decide to be a designer you must start to build your own career. You can't go back and assist, and I've told this to everybody who's assisted me. After **The**

01–02 **Catch Me If You Can**
starring Leonardo DiCaprio

Hudsucker Proxy, I told everybody I knew, "If anything comes up, I'm ready to design." When Judy was offered a college comedy called **PCU** (1994), she recommended me for the job. It was 18 years ago, but feels like yesterday; I was so excited and I had the greatest time designing that movie. **Dumb & Dumber** (1994) provided a huge leap in my career. Director Peter Farrelly told me that he had interviewed many designers whose work he'd never seen. He liked the movies that I'd assisted on, which gave him enough confidence about my work to hire me. When New Line Cinema signed Jim Carrey for a record seven million dollars they told Farrelly, "You can hire a different designer, you don't have to use this girl who has designed one or two movies." Luckily for me Peter said, "No, I want Zophres."

Richard Hornung was set to design **Fargo** (1996) on location in Minnesota after **City Hall** (1996). Very ill, he went into the hospital and he didn't want to leave his doctor in New York. The Coens asked him, "We're brokenhearted, but who do you recommend?" Heart racing and hugely nervous, I flew myself to New York for the meeting. They offered me the movie, and I screamed, "Oh my God!" and they just started laughing. And after **Fargo**, they asked me to design **The Big Lebowski** (1998).

I was designing **Any Given Sunday** (1999) for Oliver Stone, when I got the call to design **O Brother, Where Art Thou?** (2000). Many directors would have found someone who'd already designed a 1930s' movie, but that didn't even occur to the Coens. They feel that I am capable of designing anything that they write. I'll be forever grateful for that confidence. I spent every weekend thinking about **O Brother, Where Art Thou?** The Coens' scripts have a certain style; they write so vividly and evocatively, that I know how I want them to look. By chance, I found a book of photographs called *One Time, One Place: Mississippi in the Depression* by Eudora Welty. The sepia tone, the hot sweaty looseness, the sack quality and the silhouette of the clothes in the novel captured the feeling of the movie. Turning the pages, I knew that this is how →

O BROTHER, WHERE ART THOU?
(03–04) "One of the challenges on **O Brother, Where Art Thou?** was how to make George Clooney look like Everett, the hayseed that he was playing. It was not an easy task, but that's how I landed upon the idea of overalls; I loved the back straps. These overalls were a replica of a very early pair that we found in the historic Dykeman-Young Collection. Holly Hunter (Penny) is so petite that she fit in all original vintage dresses from the time period **(04)**."

TRUE GRIT

(01–02) "Rooster's (Jeff Bridges) 'Ulster' coat was an item that I was obsessed with, but could not find a prototype in stock anywhere. That's when my cutter, Celeste Cleveland, came to the rescue and made it in 32-ounce wool for Jeff's first fitting from a photo from my research. Jeff put on the coat and there was Rooster in the fitting room." (03–04) "What's meant to be Mattie's (Hailee Steinfeld) father's overcoat, is made out of 22-ounce greenish-brown textured wool. The leather belt that is cinched around her waist was meant to have come off her father's saddlebag. She wears her father's grey wool trousers and his 'boss of the plains' style hat with a 4″ brim and 4″ crown. A little peek of femininity appears at her collar; Mattie's own blouse and her own button hook boots. Every girl working on the set wanted this outfit. We all wanted to tuck our high-waisted trousers (with suspenders) in our boots and wear an oversized coat cinched at the waist."

> **"My theory is, the minute that you decide to be a designer you must start to build your own career. You can't go back and assist."**

O Brother, Where Art Thou? should look. Whether it's a contemporary or period film, I always start with research. It doesn't have to be picking up a 1920s' or 1930s' catalog and studying the clothes, but I need some kind of visual reference. We didn't have enough budget or staff on **O Brother, Where Art Thou?**, but I loved designing that movie.

For **Iron Man 2** (2010) I did a set of renderings for director Jon Favreau, who said, "What is this?" I'm a decent sketch artist, but Jon was used to computer-rendered photos with realistic 3D effects, like those created for **Iron Man** (2008). I reassured him that, "My illustrator Christian Cordella will do them," and I didn't draw any more sketches myself. Marvel had to see and approve them, so that was different for me, but they were fine with Christian's work and they loved the character of Black Widow.

When I first got the script for the Coen brothers' **True Grit** (2010), I really had to brush up on that 19th-century time period although I could recognize the "look" from my art history background. I read a lot because I wanted to understand the context, not only historically, but also in the diaries and letters from women and men of the time. I found a lot of the written text to be more helpful than the photographs, which were often taken in studios where they were sometimes wearing the studio's clothes. After two months of research, I was so completely embedded in this world that I could design the film.

I was designing **True Grit** when director Jon Favreau offered me **Cowboys & Aliens** (2011). The casting on **True Grit** was late, and we were scrambling. Twelve or 15 multiples of each costume had to be made and aged, and we only had three people working with us when we needed ten. So, I turned down **Cowboys & Aliens**. Stacey Snider, the head of DreamWorks, said, "Whatever it takes, get her on it." I came up with ridiculous demands. I said, "I need my tailor shop..." because I was going to Austin to do the Texas part of **True Grit**. "I need my cutter/fitter. I need an ager/dyer in Austin to help me dye...

And I need an illustrator," because I knew at that point that Jon Favreau didn't get my drawings, so I needed Christian Cordella, "and a researcher, and they all have to come to Texas."

They said, "Yes." Them saying yes was such a big ego boost for me that I was like "Okay, I'll do it." Honestly, it was hell because I was working 15-hour days on **True Grit**, then I'd stay for two or three hours working on **Cowboys & Aliens**, then go home and go to sleep for four hours, then get up and start all over again. I worked every weekend. It was brutal.

Directors who inspire me like the Coens make me feel very lucky. I love telling the story and I think I'm very fortunate that I get to work with the Coens who provide the perfect environment in which I can blossom. But I also enjoy myself working with Jon Favreau or with Steven Spielberg. A designer has to be able to engage and I love the collaboration of it all. It's also very important to love actors and to love the process of turning them into their characters and I do— especially character actors. Jeff Bridges is the perfect example. It's really fun to see him transform in the fitting room.

I would love to design a fantasy film or something Elizabethan, which is completely out of my safety zone; that would be a welcome challenge. My favorite pastime with my husband is going somewhere to people-watch. I'll see somebody walking down the street and I just try to imagine what their entire closet looks like and I imagine what they wear on a daily basis. That all goes back to working in the clothing store. It's not about fashion, it's about identity; the way someone wears their clothes indicates how they feel about themselves. It helps to evoke the characters that are written on the page. That's why I do costume design. I don't do costume design because I like fashion. I've never been particularly interested in fashion except when I'm designing a contemporary movie where someone has to look fabulous. I do costume design because I love movies. I feel lucky; I've been designing for 18 years now and I love what I do. I love telling the story.

Research, research, research

(01–04) "In **No Country for Old Men** I wanted Anton (Javier Bardem) to be dark and menacing, and out of place in the environment of West Texas. He was the darkest end of the palette in the movie **(01)**. His custom-made boots have a very pointy toe out of a creepy crocodile skin. I wanted the boots to be another weapon for him. The design for his distinctive haircut came from a research photo from a 'prisoner/convict' file from the Warner Brothers research library." **(02, 04)** Zophres' extensive research process comes together in a mood board of visual references for each character in the film she is working on.

Shirley Russell

Born in 1935 in Woodford, Essex, Shirley showed signs of her artistic talent at an early age. "When I was about ten years old my father used to say to me, 'You waste all your time drawing ladies.' But it was really the clothes on the ladies that I was drawing—outlining the figures and then filling them in with beautiful costumes." Recognizing her propensity for design, Shirley attended art school "to learn properly: dress design and pattern cutting." It was there that she met her future husband, the late filmmaker Ken Russell. "The photography students used to try to persuade the dress-design students to model for them and the dress-design students in turn used to try to persuade the photographers to take pictures of their clothes." Then, she attended the Royal College of Art: "I started there on a fashion course and I think it was then I decided that I hated fashion. I was much more interested in the history of fashion. I got out of fashion and into costume design."

In the mid 1950s, the Russells started a family and started to make amateur films. On the strength of their shorts **Peep Show** (1956) and **Amelia and the Angel** (1959), Ken started directing feature films and Shirley served as his costume designer and his creative partner. She noted, "We're always discussing ideas for films, it's not as much him as us, really. When we start shooting a film my role as costume designer is enough. I haven't time to do anything more. It's all-embracing." Ken declared: "I couldn't be making films without my wife."

Women in Love (1969) and **The Devils** (1971) were two of their early successes. The ground-breaking and often shocking content of the films was grounded by Shirley's attention to the styling of historic garments. "With **Women in Love**, my idea was to get everything as genuinely 1919 as possible, right down to the garters. Even if they were never going to be seen, I'd always insist that the girls wore everything so the clothes would hang right—it helps the actors get into the part." For **The Devils**, "where you can't possibly find any 17th-century costumes, it's very tempting to stylize, then stylize a bit more."

01 Shirley Russell with her then-husband the late Ken Russell (1969)

02 Women in Love

03 Lisztomania

04 Reds

05 Valentino (1977)

06 The Devils

03

The Russells made 15 films together into the 1970s, including **The Boy Friend** (1971), **Tommy** (1975) and **Lisztomania** (1975). She opined: "I've been lucky, going through the whole spectrum from realism to fantasy." After they divorced in 1978, Shirley continued to work for other directors and designed **Agatha** (1979) and **Reds** (1981), receiving Oscar nominations for both. She also designed **Hope and Glory** (1987), **Enigma** (2001), and several TV movies for director Charles Sturridge until she died in 2002. Sturridge summed Shirley up, "Although she was a detailed researcher, she wasn't a literalist. She understood clothing as one element of storytelling and looked for items that allowed insight into character." He added, "Actors always said that working with Shirley wasn't like choosing costumes, it was like picking out your character's wardrobe." Shirley concluded, "I'd hate anybody in the audience to be more aware of the costume than of the actor."

Glossary

Above the Line The salaries of the director, writer, producer and actors, including profit participation. "**Below the Line**" refers to all other production expenses including the crew. Costume designers are below the line and do not receive additional money from the profit of the film.

Arc The narrative and emotional path of each character in a story. Costumes must embody each character's journey during the film.

Assistant Costume Designer Indispensible, their many creative responsibilities include, interfacing with the cutter, shopping and pulling costumes. They are the designer's eyes and ears in meetings and on the set.

Atmosphere (or **Extras**) Non-principal players in a scene—crowd, pedestrians, diners, the appropriate people needed to populate the screen.

Atmosphere Call The notice to extra casting. The type of people, socially and economically, that are needed for that day of production.

Background Talent Another way of saying "extras" or "atmosphere."

Bits When a background player, or extra, is featured in a scene, like a waiter. A "silent bit" may be an elevator operator who may be featured with no dialogue.

Blocking The choreography of a scene. The ground may be chalked or taped in coordination with the camera angle or movement.

Break-Away A specially rigged costume that tears in the scene. Several are made to accommodate more than one "take."

Call Sheet Distributed to all cast and crew every day that informs everyone of the actors, crew and logistics required to continue production the next day of shooting and includes the "advance" schedule for the following days.

Call Time When cast and crew are needed to arrive on the set. Call time varies for each department. It is not unusual for the costume department to be the first to arrive on the set and the last to leave on any shooting day.

CGI (Computer Generated Effects) Any digital effect including computer animation, removal of wires, weather effects, flying effects, and additional atmosphere.

Cinematographer Director of photography (DOP/DP) is responsible for lighting the movie. The camera operator actually operates the camera and the gaffer runs the electrical department that provides light to the set.

Color Palette The costume designer, production designer and the cinematographer work closely with the director to determine a color palette for the film.

Continuity Book The collected notes kept by the script supervisor of each and every shot of every scene in the film. Films are not shot in chronological order. Continuity is a vital tool in post-production for the film editor who will assemble these thousands of pieces of footage.

Costume Bible A volume of collected research including photographs, sketches, hair and makeup notes, inspiration, memoirs, fabric and color swatches. It may be shared with the director, production designer, actors and the hair and makeup artists. Some designers create websites as with research online, available to all collaborators and actors as needed.

Costume Breakdown The costume changes for every single character in every scene. Including day, week, year and seasonal changes in the script in addition to action scenes in which multiple costumes will be needed. The budget is based on the type and number of costumes needed.

Costume Every piece of clothing worn in a movie is a costume whether that garment is borrowed, rented, purchased, or designed and created especially for the film. Those films with no custom-made garments are still "designed." Each piece is chosen, altered and aged for the character, the story and composition of the frame.

Costume Designer Other than the actor, the costume designer is most responsible for bringing the people in the story to life. The artistry of the costume designer lies in the creation of the unique individuals who people the script.

Costume Designers Guild, Local 892 Covers costume designers in Los Angeles. www.costumedesignersguild.com

Costume Plot Each character's costume is broken down by scene and numbered chronologically. Costume change numbers become all the more complicated during long chase scenes and action sequences when there are multiple units shooting and when there are practical special effects.

Costume Plot Pro A digital software program for prepping, running, and budgeting a costume department for a film or television series primarily used by costume supervisors.

Costume Sketch (Costume Design UK) After reading the script the costume designer may develop ideas digitally or on paper. If the designer is too busy on the production or the sketch requires a slick finish (such as a super-hero) they may work with a costume illustrator. Many designers choose to use mood boards, collages of inspiration as communication tools. Whether or not sketches are created is ultimately irrelevant. The characters on screen define the "art of costume."

Costume Stock The general store of costumes at the studio or costume rental house. It is a unparalleled resource for the designer and set costumers to pick and "pull" modern and period clothes for extras and principal actors.

Costume Supervisor The managing director of the costume department and the close partner of the designer. Their responsibilities include overseeing the shopping and manufacture of the costumes and the transportation needs of the department. The costume supervisor leads the set crew and acts as the chief financial officer of the department. They support the costume designer with managerial and organizational skills.

Costumer An essential part of the costume crew with many responsibilities, including dressing the actors, ironing, laundry, continuity, assisting in the fittings and creating the costume department on location. Dedication to the designer's vision and incredible stamina is the hallmark of a great and generous crew.

Costumier Theater costume designer (UK).

Cutter/Fitter Their artistry is crucial to the costume designer whose own work depends upon the talent and loyalty of their crew. Cutters and tailors transform an average design into a work of art using their skill, experience and imagination. They enhance every costume by suggesting the most amenable fabric, lining and trims. Designers form long-term partnerships with cutter-fitters they trust.

Dance Rubber Applied to the soles of actor's shoes to prevent slipping and sliding with the additional advantage of silencing foot falls.

Day Check An additional costumer who is called in for one day to help dress atmosphere.

Day Out of Days The master-shooting schedule created by the first assistant director.

Day Player An actor who has one or two lines in a film and works one day.

Deal Memo The personal agreement that a costume designer makes with the production as differentiated from the union contract. It may include the placement of credit, the length and terms of employment and salary, travel, accommodation and "kit" rental. It will change over a designer's career and reflect the variables of the marketplace.

Distressing (Aging/Breaking Down) An old Hollywood expression for aging the costumes by helping the clothes look "lived in" and essential for creating authentic characters. Aging is accomplished by sandpaper, sponges, spray bottles, steel brushes, awls, dye, bleaching (fading), glue, spray paint, matches, cigarette lighters, motor oil, cooking oil, food coloring, Kensington gore (movie blood), and Fuller's earth (sterile movie dirt). There are also useful commercial wax crayons available like "Schmutzstik" and "Schmere" for an on-set kit.

Draping After the fabric is draped on the dress form (dummy UK) artfully with pins it is marked and removed. A flat pattern for the garment is created from the marked fabric.

Dresser The person who dresses actors in the theater. In cinema, costumers dress the actors.

Establishing a Costume The first time a costume is worn on film (this can be completely out of chronological continuity). The costume designer will be on set to insure the director approves it on the actor. The costume change will be then "set in stone" for the rest of the shoot to match the continuous action.

Fashion in Film There is no fashion in film, these terms are mutually exclusive. Each accessory and garment that a character wears has a unique history in the same way that our own clothes have histories. Clothes in the movies take third place to character and story.

First A.D. The first assistant director is the floor manager of the set. He or she is in charge of all departments making sure that everything is ready for the director.

Fitting Room Can be a character laboratory where new people are invented through experimentation and collaboration between the actor and the costume designer.

Key Costumer The lead costumer working on the set who works directly under the costume supervisor. Entrusted with the look of the scene after the costume designer "establishes" the clothes for the first time on the actors.

Kit Rental Paid by the production, "kit" may include a smart phone, a laptop computer and tablet, a printer, scanner, art supplies, vintage jewelry, clothing and fabrics, research, all the specialized tools that a costumer and designer bring with them. Kit rental may also offset stalled salary negotiations and add cash into a deal memo when the weekly salary is reduced.

Line Producer A line producer deals with the nuts and bolts of production as differentiated from the producer who raised the original financing for the film.

Line-by-Line Read Through Where the cast and crew sit together around a big table when the dialogue and all stage directions are read aloud so that everyone knows exactly what is required for each scene.

Loss and Damage A line item in a costume budget that can provide helpful padding for the designer, it also covers loss and damage.

MoCap Motion Capture records the movements of actors who are connected to digital cameras and turned into animated characters pioneered by directors Robert Zemekis, James Cameron and Peter Jackson.

Multiples Required protection for perspiration, loss and damage, weather, continuity and aging, stunt doubles, second and third units, squibs, and action sequences. Multiple garments (replacements) means the director never has to wait for a shot.

Motion Picture Costumers, Local 705 Local covering costumers in Los Angeles. www.motionpicturecostumers.org

ND Nondescript or neutral fabric or clothing that is meant to disappear.

Over-the-Shoulder A shot over the actor's shoulder during a conversation in a scene.

Period Any time in the past other than the present. It is sometimes confusing that modern costumes are considered period clothes when the setting is just a few years past.

Ponce Bags Cheesecloth bags created to hold Fuller's Earth. Allows for a costumer to dust the shoulders, clothes and boots of the actor. Fuller's Earth labels reflect the landscape such as Monument Valley Red, often used in Westerns.

Post-Production The process after the last "take" has been printed. "Post" includes wrap, editing, sound mixing and Foley, dubbing and looping (more sound), music and music scoring, special effects, color timing and printing the film.

POV The character's "point of view," what they see.

Pre-Fit The atmosphere players or extras are fitted by the costume designer, costume supervisor and costumer, weeks or days before they are needed for shooting. Their sizes are sent from casting to the second assistant director and then to the costume supervisor. Under the supervision of the costume designer, the crew will pull the costumes from costume stock for the pre-fit day. The designer and the crew will accessorize the costumes with hats, gloves, bags, jewelry and coats prior to the arrival of the extras. These ensembles will be sized and arranged by color on the rack (rail UK). In this way, the designer can keep strict control of the color palette for each scene.

Prep The time that the designer and the crew is given to shop, design, manufacture and prepare the costumes for the production up until the first day of shooting.

Product Placement When a company seeks to place a product prominently in a scene in a narrative film (not a commercial) to promote their product. Sometimes they also offer cash to off-set production costs. A minefield for designers trying to create real people in a real world.

Production Designer The production designer creates the world of the story and partners with the set dresser to furnish each scene with a background and objects that provide the audience with details regarding the time and circumstances in which the story takes place.

Props Something that an actor uses during a scene, a cigarette, a coffee cup, a briefcase, or a newspaper. Historically, props provide wedding bands, watches and glasses and the costume designer chooses the appropriate one for each character.

Rushes (Dailies) Directors, department heads, and studio executives are emailed the footage from the previous day's shooting from the editor. This is the opportunity a department head has to see their day's work on film and evaluate if it may be improved.

Scale (Costume Designers Contract US) The base fee for a costume designer is the lowest of the creative department heads. The current scale for the costume designer in the US is 30 percent less than for a production designer of the same experience. Designers may negotiate a deal memo above scale. However, the very low scale for costume designers underscores the dramatic historic gender bias that continues in the film industry.

Shooting Schedule This is the order in which scenes will be shot in a film including the season, the weather, the locations and the time of day.

Shopping Costume designers must know who a character is before they can shop for them. Every film uses shopped, rented, altered and/or designed and manufactured costumes. Modern films are among the most difficult to design because everyone has an opinion and the actor may confuse their own taste from that of the character.

Squib A squib is a small explosive (pyrotechnic) used to simulate a bullet hit. These can be placed in costumes, walls, or props.

Stand-ins Professionals of the same height and coloring of the principal actors who stand-in while the cameraman lights the scene. Sometimes they are asked to wear the same color clothes as the principal costume.

Stunt Double Replaces the actor if the action requires a special skill (like horseback riding) or places the actor in harm's way.

Swatches Fabric color changes under natural and artificial light. Swatches of fabric are gathered to determine which will work best for each character, scene and color palette. These are shared with the production designer and sometimes the cinematographer.

Teching (Dipping Costumes) Over-dyeing fabric to create an ivory or warm tech or with a charcoal stain to create a pale gray fabric to modify the brightness and reflectivity of a white shirt or costume.

Toile (Muslin US) The cutter-fitter will create a toile out of inexpensive fabric. This is the first three-dimensional interpretation of the design whether from a sketch or a conversation. The designer will correct the toile on the dress form. Then, a final flat pattern will be made.

Toupee Tape Invisible two-sided tape used on delicate skin or fabric.

Two-Shot (Tight/Wide) Two actors featured in the frame.

U.P.M. A Unit Production Manager is responsible for the budget and schedule of the film on a day-to-day basis.

Union Film Where the crew is working under a contract negotiated by a labor union, like the IATSE (International Alliance of Theatrical and Stage Employees) and the employers (the studios.) Non–union salaries may equal union salaries. The difference is the pension and health benefits the producer must put aside for the employee. Costume locals exist to protect the working conditions, hours and wages of their membership.

United Scenic Artists, Local 829 The New York local that covers costume designers on the east coast of the United States. www.usa829.org

Wardrobe A wooden chest to keep clothing. This archaic term is still widely used and was a term of derision for many years. "Wardrobe" people are costume professionals who prefer the word "costume."

Wide-Shot The actors will be seen from head to foot.

Work for Hire Costume designers do not own anything that they create for a film. They do not own their designs and are not paid, remunerated or credited when those designs are licensed for dolls, video games, Halloween costumes, sequels, or copied seam for seam by fashion designers. Costume designers have no possessory label. Many designers (of film franchises) have tried to negotiate a deal for the merchandising of their designs with the studios and production companies. With modest exceptions these efforts have failed.

Wrap The end of every day of filming when the departments clean and put away their equipment. Costumes are broken down (separated, tagged with the name of the actor and laundered). The final wrap involves cleaning the costumes and drawing up an inventory, returning rentals, paying bills, and shipping principal costumes into storage to a costume house, a studio or production company. These are kept together for possible reshoots. After the film has had its commercial release, costumes may be sold to the public by eBay or auction, sold to costume rental houses for stock, placed in costume stock at the studio. Only a lucky few are kept safe in a studio archive.

Picture Credits

Courtesy of Jenny Beavan: 18B, 20TL, 20TR; Photograph by Rolf Konow: 14.

BFI Stills Collection: 186L.

Courtesy of Yvonne Blake: 28TR, 31R, 32C, 33BL; Photograph by David Carretero: 24.

Courtesy of Mark Bridges: 38TL, 38TR, 39B, 43T, 44L, 45TR, 45BR; Photograph by Claudette Barius: 34.

Courtesy of Shay Cunliffe: 50TR, 50BR; Photograph by Mary Cybulski: 48.

Courtesy of Sharen Davis/Illustration by Gina Flanagan: 66TL, 66TC, 66TR; Illustration by Felipe Sanchez: 63L.

Getty Images/Frazer Harrison: 58; E. Neitzel: 176.

Courtesy of Aggie Guerard Rodgers/Photograph by David Bornfriend: 134; Illustration by Haleen Holt: 143BL, 143BR.

Courtesy of Lindy Hemming: 68, 70, 71TL, 73BR, 74L, 77TR, 77BR.

Courtesy of Joanna Johnston: 80; Illustration by Robin Richesson: 84R, 85T, 88B, 89B.

Courtesy of Michael Kaplan: 93L, 93R, 96T, 101TR; Illustration by Pauline Annon: 96BR, 97BL, 97CR; Photograph by David James: 90; Illustration by Brian Valenzuela: 95TL, 95BL, 98.

The Kobal Collection: 112L; 20th Century Fox: 56, 79L, 97TC, 101L, 105B, 132, 137BL, 152TR, 152BR, 175T, 175BL; 20th Century Fox/Brian Hamill: 107TR; 20th Century Fox/Merrick Morton: 6, 97BR; 20th Century Fox/Stephen Vaughan: 101BR; Antena 3 TV/Saul Zaentz Productions: 28B; Beacon/Dirty Hands: 151; Carolco: 127; Carolco/Canal +/Rcs Video: 126T; Castle Rock: 54T; Castle Rock Entertainment/John Clifford: 52; Castle Rock/Shangri-La Entertainment: 89T; Cinergi Pictures: 148; Columbia: 26, 27, 33T, 53L, 78BR, 136, 144BL, 145L; Columbia/Bob Coburn: 113R; Columbia/Merchant Ivory: 19B; Columbia/Zade Rosenthal: 67; Danjaq/Eon/UA/Keith Hampshere: 73T; De Line Pictures: 5, 95BR, 95TR; Dreamworks LLC: 159TR, 159BR; Dreamworks LLC/David James: 87BL; Dreamworks Pictures: 66CL, 66BL, 66BR; Dreamworks SKG: 87T; Dreamworks SKG/Universal/Karen Ballard: 83; Dreamworks/Andrew Cooper: 180R; Dreamworks/Suzanne Hanover: 165; Dreamworks/Universal/Jaap Buitendijk: 172, 173; Edward R. Pressman Film: 133BC, 133BR; Epsilon/20th Century Fox/Rico Torres: 120TL; Film Trust Production: 31BL, 31TL; Fine Line/Medusa/Sergio Strizzi: 118; Focus Features: 160TR; Geffen/Warner Bros: 138; Ghoulardi/New Line/Revolution/Bruce Birmelin: 42; Grosvenor Park Productions: 23; Icon Productions/Marquis Films/Antonello, Phillipe: 21T; Icon/Warner Bros: 117L, 117R; Imagine/Universal/Eli Reed: 36; ITV Global: 30; La Classe Americaine/Ufilm/France 3: 45TL; Ladd Company/Warner Bros: 92, 93C; Lucasfilm/20th Century Fox: 140; Lucasfilm/Coppola Co/Universal: 137TR; Lucasfilm/Coppola Co/Universal: 137TL; Mandalay Ent/Paramount/Alex Bailey: 170; Mandeville Films: 41BR, 41BL; Mandeville Films/Jojo Whilden: 41T; Medusa/Pacific/Miramax: 119; Merchant Ivory: 16; Merchant Ivory/Goldcrest: 17; MGM: 79R, 137BR; MGM/Eon/Keith Hamshere: 73BL; MGM/Mandeville/Sam Emerson: 60; MGM/Ron Phillips: 37T; MGM/UA: 57TL, 57TR, 130R, 150; Mike Zoss Productions: 178; Miramax/Dimension Films/Paul Chedlow: 122T; Miramax/Dimension Films/Peter Sore: 162T; New Line: 39TR, 53R, 65B, 94; New Line/Avery Pix/Lorey Sebastian: 2, 37B; New Line/G Lefkowitz: 39TL; New Line/Ralph Nelson Jnr: 108R, 109; New Line/Jaimie Trueblood: 120TC; P.E.A.: 47BL; P.E.A./Artistes Associes: 47TL; Paramount: 47R, 71TR, 84L, 85BL, 96BL, 126B, 131TR, 131B, 153, 187TR; Paramount/Bad Robot: 99; Paramount/Philip Caruso: 85BR; Paramount/Miramax: 185TL, 185BL; Paramount/Melissa Moseley: 158; Paramount/Vantage: 43B; Picturehouse: 40; Polygram/Channel 4/Working Title: 74R, 75;

Polygram/Frank Masi: 33BR; Polygram/Joss Barratt: 169; Polygram/Philip Caruso: 164; Scott Rudin Productions: 44R; See-Saw Films: 19TR, 19TL; Silver Pictures: 20B; Skydance Productions: 182R; Skydance Productions/Lorey Sebastian: 183R; Sony Pictures Entertainment: 50L, 51; Spelling/Price/Savoy: 152L; Thin Man/Greenlight: 71B; Touchstone: 88T; Touchstone Pictures/Jerry Bruckheimer Films/Jonathan Hession: 154; Touchstone/Amblin: 87BR; Touchstone/Buena Vista Pictures/Doane Gregory: 18T; Touchstone/Universal: 181B; Touchstone/Universal/Melina Sue Gordon: 181T; TriStar: 62L, 160CR; TriStar/Carolco: 129R; TriStar/Murray Close: 105T; TriStar/Firooz Zahedi: 62R; United Artists: 78TR, 86, 144BR, 145R, 186R, 187CR; United Artists/Fantasy Films: 139; United Artists/Seven Arts: 112R; Universal: 46L, 64, 65TR, 65TL, 82, 113L, 163B; Universal/Francois Duhamel: 110BR, 110T; Universal/Jasin Boland: 55; Universal/Joseph Lederer: 128T, 128B; Universal/Scott Free: 174; USA Films/Capitol Films/Film Council: 22B; USA Films/Capitol Films/Film Council/Mark Tillie: 22T; VMG/Austral. Film Finance/BR Screen: 179R; Walt Disney Pictures: 149TR, 149BL, 155, 160L; Walt Disney Pictures/Stephen Vaughan: 149TL; Warner Bros: 54B, 104R, 142, 143TR, 143TL, 187BR, 187L; Warner Bros/Channel 4/Jaap Buitendijk: 171; Warner Bros/DC Comics: 32R, 32L, 77L; Warner Bros/Merie W. Wallace: 57B; Warner Bros/Murray Close: 104L; Warner Bros/Stephen Vaughan: 141; Weinstein Co: 61, 161; Wildwood/Allied Filmmakers/David James: 111B, 111TR; Zanuck Independent: 163TL, 163TR.

Courtesy of Judianna Makovsky: 106, 107BL, 107TL, 108L, 110BL, 111TL; Photograph by April Rocha: 102.

Courtesy of Maurizio Millenotti: 114, 120TR, 120BR, 120BL, 121BL, 121BR, 122C, 122B.

Courtesy of Ellen Mirojnick: 124, 129L, 133TL, 133TR; Illustration by Christian Cordella: 131TL, 131TC; Illustration by Lois DeArmond: 130L; Illustration by Sara O'Donnell: 133BL.

Courtesy of the family of Ruth Morley: 144T.

Photofest/Metro-Goldwyn-Mayer: 78L; New Line Cinema: 38B; United Artists: 46R.

Rex Features/Everett Collection: 28TL.

Courtesy of Penny Rose: 146; Illustration by Darrell Warner: 149BR.

Courtesy of Julie Weiss: 159L, 162BL, 162BR; Photograph by Mark Garland: 156.

Courtesy of Janty Yates: 166; Photograph by Kerry Brown: 174TL; Illustration by Lora Revitt: 174TR, 175BR.

Courtesy of Mary Zophres/Courtesy of Miramax. All Rights Reserved: 179L; Courtesy of Paramount Pictures © 2002 DW Studios LLC. All Rights Reserved: 180L; © 2010 Paramount Pictures. All Rights Reserved: 182L, 183L; © 2007 by Paramount Vantage, a Division of Paramount Pictures and Miramax Film Corp. All Rights Reserved: 185TR, 185BR.

Special thanks to Lauretta Dives, Caroline Bailey, Dave Kent, Darren Thomas, Phil Moad, and Cheryl Thomas at The Kobal Collection for all of their effort and support.

Index